THE Kailas at ELLORA

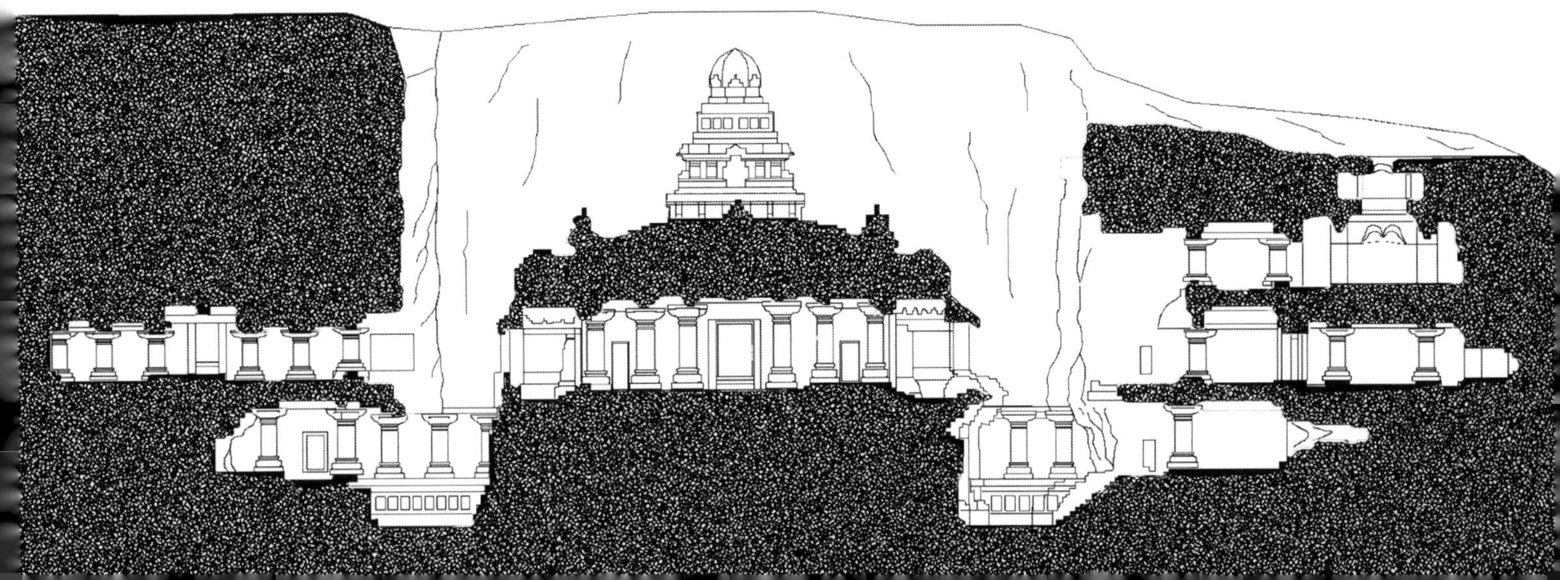

THE Kailas at ELLORA

A New View of a Misunderstood Masterwork

Roger Vogler

with photographs by
Peeyush Sekhsaria and **Roger Vogler**

INTACH
Aurangabad

Mapin Publishing

PAGE 2
Ravana shaking Mount Kailasa, south wall of Vimana

PAGE 5
River Goddess Ganga, Ellora Cave 21

PAGES 6-7
First glimpse of Gajalakshmi sculpture (see page 26)

First published in India in 2015 by
INTACH Aurangabad
B-5, MIDC Area, Near Railway Station,
Aurangabad 431005

in association with

Mapin Publishing
706 Kaivanna, Panchvati, Ellisbridge,
Ahmedabad 380006 INDIA

Simultaneously published in the United States of America in 2015 by
Grantha Corporation
77 Daniele Drive, Hidden Meadows, Ocean Township, NJ 07712
E: mapin@mapinpub.com

Distributed in North America by
Antique Collectors' Club
T: +1 800 252 5231 • F: 413 529 0862
E: info@antiquecc.com
www.antiquecollectorsclub.com

Distributed in United Kingdom and Europe by
Gazelle Book Services Ltd.
T: +44 1 5246 8765 • F: 44 1524 63232
E: sales@gazellebooks.co.uk
www.gazellebookservices.co.uk

Distributed in Thailand, Laos, Cambodia and Myanmar by
Paragon Asia Co. Ltd
T: +66 2877 7755 • F: 66 2468 9636
E: info@paragonasia.com

Distributed in Malaysia by
Areca Books
T: + 604 2610307
E: arecabooks@gmail.com

Distributed in the Rest of the World by
Mapin Publishing Pvt. Ltd
T: +91 79 40 228 228 • F: +91 79 40 228 201
E: mapin@mapinpub.com
www.mapinpub.com

Roger Vogler and Peeyush Sekhsaria wish to extend their grateful thanks to the Architectural Survey of India for their for their generous permission and assistance in photographing the Kailas.

ISBN: 978-81-89995-86-7 (Mapin)
ISBN: 978-1-935677-42-0 (Grantha)
LCCN: 2015940507

Copyediting: Neha Manke and Ankona Das / Mapin Editorial
Design: Gopal Limbad / Mapin Design Studio
Production Assistance: Rakesh Manger / Mapin Design Studio
Printed at Parksons Graphics, Mumbai

INTACH Aurangabad would like to express its gratitude to following companies for their support in bringing out this publication

Endress + Hauser Flowtec (India) Pvt. Ltd

Endress + Hauser Automation Instrumentation Pvt. Ltd

Endurance Technologies Pvt. Ltd

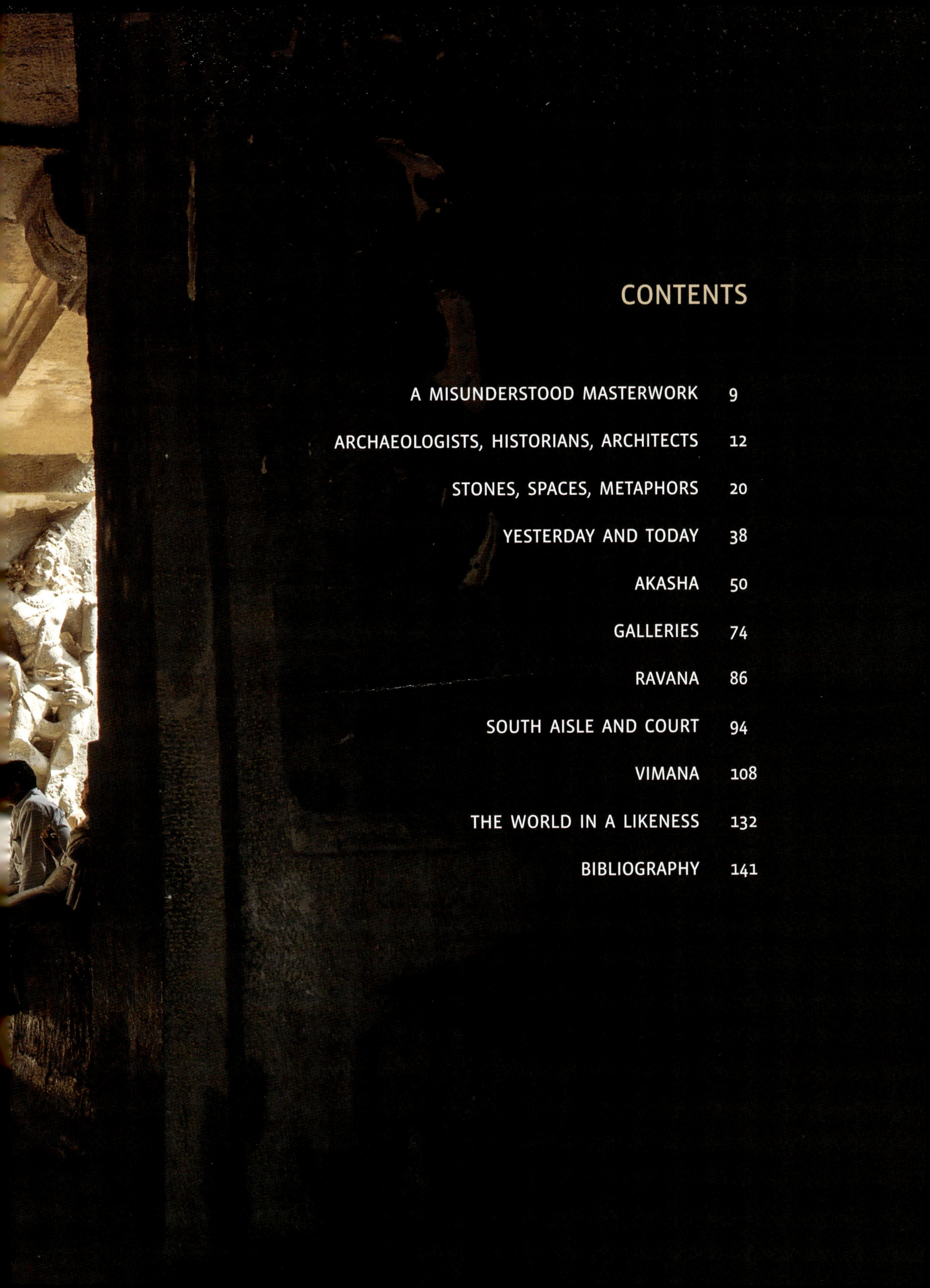

CONTENTS

Based upon Survey of India maps with the permission of the Surveyor General of India. ©2015, Government of India. Responsibility for the correctness of internal details shown on the main map rests with the publisher.

A Misunderstood Masterwork

I am an architect by training and experience. Soon after arriving in India in August 1968, to begin a three-year assignment as design consultant for the new campus of IIT-K (Indian Institute of Technology, Kanpur), I visited the World Heritage cave temple site of Ellora. Its principal monument is the eighth-century Hindu temple called Kailasa, or, simply, the Kailas. It is not a cave in the usual sense, however: instead of being carved laterally into the face of a cliff, it was carved downward from the top of one. Or more specifically, a huge temple of primeval stone was left standing free, complete in every detail, in the middle of an excavation the size of a football field [figure 1].

Moving through the Kailas that first time, as a new view of its magnificent stone carving unfolded at every step, splayed against an omnipresent background of towering raw cliffs, was the most exhilarating and powerful architectural expression of space I had ever experienced. It remains so today.

Thirty-seven years were to pass before I saw the Kailas again. Its spatial impact was just as I remembered it. But this time, with the knowledge and understanding of Hinduism that I had gained over those intervening years, superficial as it remains, I had come to realize that its spatial qualities are only a fraction of what this temple has to offer—to a visitor open enough in spirit truly to see and feel it. To experience the Kailas fully, one must open one's senses to *see* its forms, to *feel* its space, and to *comprehend* the profound conceptions that lie beneath their surface, hidden in metaphor.

Kailasa is a real mountain that rises dramatically from the Tibetan plain, beyond the high Himalayas. Isolated, strikingly formed, perpetually snow-capped, it was a major landmark on the fabled Silk Road, the caravan route that from before the birth of Christ linked Xian in China with ancient Tyre and Antioch on the Mediterranean Sea. Mount Kailasa is sacred to Buddhists, Hindus, and Jains, and devotees of all three faiths still come from afar to tread the pilgrims' path that encircles its base, just as they have done for centuries. But

1. The Kailas panorama, looking west from atop east cliff

it is especially revered by Hindus, as the celestial abode of their great Lord Shiva.

The Kailas at Ellora, dedicated to Shiva, is a symbolic model in miniature of the real mountain, and so a microcosm of the world of the gods. Each of its many sculptures is a visual metaphor, portraying an image or tale from Hinduism's vast mythology, revealing a fundamental truth about the worlds of man and of the gods. Among these sculptural treasures is a monumental panel in high relief, located at the very base of the temple/mountain, which portrays the famous legend of Ravana shaking Mount Kailasa [see figure 39]. This evil demon was once imprisoned in the real mountain, beneath

the cave of Shiva and his consort Parvati. The demon, his ten heads alive with passion, flails his arms wildly as he attempts to topple the mountain. Above him Parvati clutches Shiva's arm for protection, her maid flees in terror, and their attendants are struck motionless in fright. Only Shiva is unperturbed, as with the slightest pressure of his toe he reduces the demon's mighty effort to naught. God, we are instructed, is all-powerful. He protects his devotees from evil. The greatest disruptions in temporal life are as nothing in the ultimate scheme of things.

It is well understood by most scholars and informed lay visitors, I believe, that this sculpture, and many others within the temple, are deliberately intended to convey metaphoric messages such as this. What is not understood, however, is that the same is true of many of the temple's architectural features, and of the ever-present raw cliff faces of the vast excavation within which the principal monument—the *vimana*—stands.

The physical forms of the temple—its individual sculptures and carved architectural details—have all been extensively documented, and the history of its creation extensively debated, by many eminent scholars, beginning with the British archaeologists James Fergusson and James Burgess in the 1870s and continuing to the present day. Concepts of *space* and *metaphor,* however, are all but totally absent from their writings. These absences have led directly, I believe, to dozens of major misunderstandings and erroneous conclusions regarding the monument itself and the intentions of its designer. I propose in this study to correct these misunderstandings and rebut these errors, one by one, in the course of a walking tour through the entire temple. Focusing not merely on its stones but on the *meanings* that lie beneath them as well, this tour will follow a route trod by thousands of devotees performing the sacred *pradakshina* (ritual circumambulation) over many centuries. By doing so, as the title suggests, I hope to shed an entirely new light on what is truly a *misunderstood masterwork* of world architecture.

Archaeologists, Historians, Architects

Before commencing this tour, however, I would like to challenge two long-held and widely accepted assumptions regarding the intentions and the identity of the Kailas's designer. The first of these, initially presented by the renowned British scholar and art historian James Fergusson in the 1870s, is that its designer chose to carve the temple downward from the top of a cliff, rather than build it conventionally from the ground up, because it was cheaper to do it that way. My second challenge aims to clarify an issue of semantics. Its purpose is not to quibble over grammar, but to put to rest a near universal—and I believe an inherently misleading—scholarly mindset as to who it was who actually *designed* the Kailas.

In his *History of Indian and Eastern Architecture*, Fergusson wrote "Almost everyone who sees [this temple] is struck with the apparently prodigious amount of labour bestowed on their excavation, and there is no doubt that their monolithic character is the principal source of the awe and wonder with which they have been regarded, and that had the Kailas been an edifice of masonry situated on the plain, it would scarcely have attracted the attention of European travellers. In reality, however, it is considerately easier and less expensive to excavate a temple than to build one...The excavating process would probably cost about one tenth of the other [but as a result] the whole has necessarily been placed in a pit."

Fergusson assumed, as is evident from this statement, that placing the temple in a "pit" was a purely economic decision on the part of its *sthapati,* and that this technique, while cost-effective, was in itself an architectural disadvantage. This assumption has since been echoed by many other scholars: his colleague James Burgess, who regarded the "pit" as an "artistic mistake;"[1] by art historian Percy Brown, writing in the 1920s, who found the temple's appearance in a "pit" "a disadvantage from which the Kailas obviously suffers;"[2] by art historian Benjamin Rowland, who asserted in the 1930s "the disadvantage of this technique is that the temple is left enshadowed at the bottom of a deep pit."[3] Many other scholars, perhaps in awe of their great predecessor's academic stature, have simply accepted

Fergusson's view without comment. Indeed, the mindset that this view of the Kailas represents pervades its scholarship at every level.

But were Fergusson and his fellow scholars correct in these evaluations?

It may indeed be true that it was less expensive to carve the temple from the top downward than to build it from the ground up. But even if so, it is by no means clear that the *sthapati*'s placement of the *vimana* 'in a pit' was an economic decision, rather than a religious or an artistic one.

In the preface to his 1876 *History of Indian and Eastern Architecture*, Fergusson wrote, "Some men of great eminence and learning, more conversant with books than buildings, have naturally drawn their knowledge and inferences from written authorities...My authorities, on the contrary, have been mainly the imperishable records in the rocks or on sculptures and carvings, which necessarily represented at the time the faith and feelings of those who executed them, and which retain their original impress to this day." Scholarly observer that he was, however, it was only these stones that he saw. What Fergusson did *not* see was the vast space that envelopes these stones, nor—as we will discover in the course of our tour—the immense power of its great raw cliffs: metaphors for the presence of God.

Diana Eck has cautioned that in a Hindu temple it is not its stones—not even the temple itself—that is important: "it is the place, the power, the manifestation of the divine...[it is] not the capacity of the gods to be present in the world, but rather the human capacity to apprehend that presence."[4] Fundamental to an understanding of the Kailas, yet rarely acknowledged in scholarly work, is the recognition that it is first and foremost a *religious* monument. The Kailas is an entire environment, within which God is metaphorically present everywhere—not by accident but by *design*. The entire temple is deliberately, purposefully designed to lead the votary through it, revealing His presence at every step through its sculpture, its architectural forms, the raw cliffs that tower above them, and not the least through the invisible space—the *akasha*—that envelops all.

The 'pit' itself, far from being a detriment, is an integral, intentional, indispensable, gut-wrenching part of this journey. Merely to stand within it, as a glance at figure 19 will confirm, is to experience one of the Kailas's most compelling images of space.

'The temple' is all of this, not merely the *vimana* at its centre. We need not be a believer to achieve this understanding—we need only to grasp what is in fact going on here: we are being manipulated: led deliberately through a succession of revelatory visual and visceral experiences. Moving through the 'pit,' hemmed in and dwarfed by massive cliffs towering overhead, is among the most powerful human experiences to be found in all of Indian art. To uncover the Kailas's mysteries we need only to open our senses and go with the flow. Their revelation cannot be achieved through an analysis, however meticulous, of its stones alone.

The second assumption I wish to challenge, also widely held, is that it was King Krishnaraja I who 'built' the Kailas. In 1883, R. G. Bandharkar and G. Ramachandra reported in the journal *Indian Antiquary* the recent discovery of a copper plate Grant dated Saka 734 (812/813 CE), unearthed while excavating for a house foundation in the city of Baroda (and thus known as the Baroda Grant). An inscription on it attributed construction of the Kailas to King Krishna I (Krishnaraja I) who ruled the Rashtrakuta Empire from 757 to 772 CE. Based on this discovery, virtually every major archaeologist or art historian who has since examined the Kailas from a holistic standpoint has presumed, directly or tacitly, that it was he who 'built' the Kailas. The fact (if we accept this evidence) that it was built under his auspices, however, does not mean that Krishna designed it. To an architect, it is abundantly clear that the planning, design and execution of this tremendously complex project was no weekend effort of an amateur, let alone of a king beset by the demands of constant military campaigns and administrative responsibilities. It was the full time job—probably extending over decades—of a professional architect. And, a superbly gifted one.

The archaeologist K. V. Soundara Rajan, who may be regarded as the dean of contemporary Kailas scholars, as he was chosen to deliver the keynote address for the 1988 Ellora Proceedings convocation at the site, refers to Krishna I as "the famed creator of the Kailasa monolith" while relegating the contribution of his architects to details of its stonework rather than to creation of an overall conception. He states, for example, "Krishna's architects had introduced...whole concepts of *Dvitala Chaturasvanas* as in the *Bhadra Sala* over the projecting porches."[5] Developing "whole concepts" of projecting porch details, however, does scant justice to the contribution of professional architects to the project. Archaeologist M. K. Dhavalikar states "Krishna I...was the builder of the Kailas," adding that "He is also credited with the conquest of the Konkan, the coastal region of western India," and that "His most noteworthy contribution was the consolidation of the vast empire stretching between the Narmada in the north and the Tungabhadra in the south."[6] Together with 'building' the Kailas on the side, he would have been a busy man indeed.

Percy Brown, an art historian writing in the 1920s, says:

> "Once the idea of the Kailas was conceived, its production became a matter of time, patience and skilled labor...That it was an expression of exalted religious emotion is obvious but even this condition could not have made such a consummation possible, had it not also had the patronage of a ruler with unlimited resources and who was at the same time moved by the loftiest ideals. This monarch has been identified as Krishna I...
>
> The first stage of the work, although laborious, was simple. It consisted in excavating out of the hillside three huge trenches at right angles cut down vertically to the level of the base of the hill, [leaving] standing in the middle a large island of rock... Beginning at the top, the process of rough-hewing the irregular mass into shape [began]...Those employed on this 'pointing' were immediately followed by the sculptors, for each portion of the carved detail appears to have been completely finished as the work progressed downward...Authorities [Brown here cites Burgess] have shown that this method of production by excavation involves much less expenditure of labour than by

> building, but on the other hand the general effect is marred by the rock production always appearing in a pit, a disadvantage from which the Kailas obviously suffers."[7]

This view excludes not only the rich sculpture and spatial excitement of its subsidiary caves, but is blind to the very feature of the Kailas that sets it apart as perhaps India's greatest work of art: the excavation itself. To make this distinction clear this study throughout refers to the free-standing central temple (including the Nandi Pavilion and five shrines encircling the *shikhara*) as the *vimana*, and uses the terms 'Kailas' or 'temple' to include the entire excavation, 'pit' and all.

Brown's assessment of the design process, at least from the perspective of an architect, absurdly underestimates its complexity. How, for instance, was a sculptor who "immediately followed" the "pointers" to know what his sculpture was to represent, what, exactly, its dimensions were to be, how it was to be oriented, and where, precisely, in three-dimensional space, it was to stand, upon or within a then featureless mass of rough stone? The ultimate result of this effort: a vast, fully articulated work of architecture, carved from a single volume of stone, must have been conceived in the mind of man—complete in every detail, with virtually no prototype for guidance—before the first workman's pick struck the top of the cliff from which it was carved. In whose mind was the Kailas conceived? And under whose guidance was it executed, in all its incredible complexity? Surely not in the mind of Krishnaraja. He was a monarch, a politician, a military general—and a busy one, as Dhavalikar has observed. Assuredly the Kailas could never have been built without his unwavering dedication to it, or without his financial support—but there is nothing to suggest that he had the time, the vision, the skills, or even the desire to create the physical form of the temple itself. Krishnaraja was the *patron* of the Kailas, just as Cosimo de'Medici was of Donatello's *David*, or Pope Julius II of Michelangelo's frescoes on the ceiling of his Sistine Chapel. All three commissioned and paid for these works. The masterpieces themselves, however, were created not by a duke, or a pope, or a monarch, but by a great sculptor, a great painter—and a great architect.

Stella Kramrisch, in her monumental study *The Hindu Temple*, gives us an idea of what was involved in the planning, site preparation, design, layout, and construction of even a conventionally built temple.[8] The work, she tells us, was traditionally entrusted to three individuals: the donor, or *yajamana* (literally 'sacrificer'), the *sthapaka*, a priest responsible for its metaphysical organization, and the *sthapati*, 'master of what stands or abides:' the architect responsible for its physical design and execution. Krishnaraja was the *yajamana* of the Kailas, but he did not design it. Its designer was an unknown *sthapati*.

A *sthapati*, according to an ancient treatise,

> should be fit to direct the construction and should be well-versed in all *Shastras*, the traditional sciences, perfect in body, righteous, kind, free from malice and jealousy, a Tantric and well-born; he should know mathematics and the *Puranas*, the ancient compendia of myths, etc., painting, and all the countries; he should be joyous, truth speaking, with senses under control, concentrated in mind, free from greed, carelessness, disease and the seven vices...famous, having firm friends and having crossed the ocean of the science of Vishnu...The temple or any other construction begun by [the *sthapaka* and the *sthapati*] should be continued by them only and by no other. In case they be not available, the work should be done by either their sons or disciples who are competent in the work.[9]

Given the likelihood that creation of the Kailas, including all of its subsidiary excavations, took place over a century or more, it was undoubtedly the work of more than a single *sthapati*. Yet from an architectural standpoint, every component of the temple complex falls logically within a single overall design conception. Perhaps the original *sthapati*'s successors were indeed his sons. In any event they were his disciples, imbued with a measure of their great predecessor's noble spirit.

Every step in the creation of a Hindu temple is rigidly governed by rules set down perhaps a millennium before Christ in the *Vedas* ('Knowledge'), collections of hymns that constitute the foundation of all Hindu thought. Every step is performed at its auspicious moment, as dictated by the positions of celestial bodies. A principal source of these rules is the *vastushastra* (*vastu* means architecture, *shastra* means treatise), found in a subtext of the *Atharvaveda*, but there are many others. "*Vastushastra*," Kramrisch tells us, "belongs to, and is, applied astrology."[10] It instructs on the selection of the site, then on its purification: seeds are planted on it, and their germination evaluated; crops are repeatedly grown to maturity and ploughed under until the earth is ritually cleansed. Offerings are made to the spirits who previously occupied the site to persuade them to depart, and the ground is purified by fire. The temple is then laid out according to a square *mandala*, an occult diagram or *yantra*, representing the universe, of which the temple is a microcosm. In the temple itself the square is the shape of its innermost sanctum, the *garbhagriha*, within which stands the symbol of God. "Proportional measurement" derived from this *mandala* "controls every dimension of the temple—the length and width of its plan, the extent of its internal spaces and even measurements of such details as doorways and base mouldings...Every part is rigorously controlled by a proportional system of measurement and interrelated by the use of a fundamental unit."[11]

Although surviving records do not tell us his name, the Kailas's *sthapati* was clearly a man of extraordinary breadth and genius. It was his responsibility to master this vast body of rules and minutiae, and to ensure the temple's spiritual efficacy by meticulous observance of its every part. But beyond this, he had to have the vision to see, hidden within this rocky hillside, the enormous building that conformed to them. For its form he had models—the Virupaksha Temple at Pattadakal (although the Kailas is twice its size), and perhaps the Kailasanatha at Kanchipuram as well—but certainly there was not even remotely a precedent for carving a building of this magnitude from solid rock, let alone from the top downward.

To an architect, the challenge of creating a tremendously complex building such as this, in which every last detail of its sculpture and architectural form had to end up precisely in its proper place, with no possibility of redoing any part of the work to correct an error, of accomplishing this without benefit of any of the simple drafting, measuring, surveying, lifting or earth-moving tools we now take for granted, and finally of adding to this task the enormous challenge of managing a work force of thousands over a period of many years, is virtually beyond comprehension.

Notes

1. Burgess, James and James Fergusson. *The Cave Temples of India*. 1880. Reprint, Delhi: Oriental Books, 1965: p. 401.
2. Brown, Percy. *Indian Architecture (Buddhist and Hindu Periods)*. Reprint, Bombay: Taraporevala, 1965: p. 74.
3. Rowland, Benjamin. *The Art & Architecture of India: Buddhist/Hindu/Jain*. Baltimore: Penguin, 1967: p. 186.
4. Eck, Diana L. *India: A Sacred Geography*. New York: Harmony Books, 2012: p. 76.
5. Soundara Rajan, K. V. *The Ellora Monoliths*. Delhi: Gian, 1988, p. 150.
6. Dhavalikar, M. K. *Masterpieces of Rashtrakuta Art*. Bombay: Taraporevala, 1983: p. 4.
7. Brown 1965, *Op. cit.*
8. Kramrisch, Stella. *The Hindu Temple*. 1946. Reprint, Delhi: Motilal Banarsidass, 1976: p. 10.
9. *Ibid.*, quoting "ancient texts."
10. *Ibid.*
11. Michell, George. *The Hindu Temple: An Introduction to Its Meaning and Forms*. New York: Harper & Row, 1977: p. 73.

Stones, Spaces, Metaphors

The Kailas is one of the thirty-odd caves carved into a low, rocky ridge that stretches north–south for several kilometres on the outskirts of the village of Ellora, in Maharashtra, 170 kilometres northeast of Mumbai. By far the largest and most complex of these caves, the Kailas is carved directly into this ridge at a right angle to it, and is thus oriented from west to east. It is entered through a tower (*gopuram*) at its west end. Its principal architectural components: the *gopuram*, Nandi Pavilion (housing the image of Shiva's mount, the bull Nandi), *mandapa* (great hall), *garbhagriha* (inner sanctum) and *shikhara* (tower) are aligned, as in most Hindu temples, along a single central axis. To the left of this string of axial spaces, and parallel to it, lie the dramatic open spaces of the North Court and North Aisle, between the *vimana* and the massive raw cliffs that form the northern edge of the temple's excavation. Carved into these cliffs are the River Goddess and Lankeshvara Caves. Parallel and to the right of the central axis are the South Court and Aisle, bounded by a similar wall of raw cliffs comprising the south edge of the excavation, into which have been carved the Paralanka and

FACING PAGE

2. Approach to the Kailas from the west

ABOVE

3. Gopuram (entrance tower)

FOLLOWING PAGE

4. Sculpted figures of Kartikeya (left), God of War, seated on his vehicle, the peacock; Agni (right) God of Fire, seated on his vehicle, the ram, on exterior of the temple's front wall

Yajnasala Caves. Due to their solar orientation, the north cliffs and their related spaces are much better lit than those on the south, where direct sunlight rarely penetrates.

The locations of all of these spaces are shown on illustrations A and B, Ground and Upper Floor Plans respectively of the temple. A few minutes' study of these plans will provide a helpful overview of the temple's general layout. But let us now begin our tour of the Kailas in earnest.

Approaching the temple across broad lawns, we face its formidable front wall, stretching left to right more than 150 feet, connecting rock outcrops at each end [figure 2]. At its centre rises an equally formidable two-story *gopuram,* or entrance tower [figure 3], through which a dark, ground level passage provides the only access into

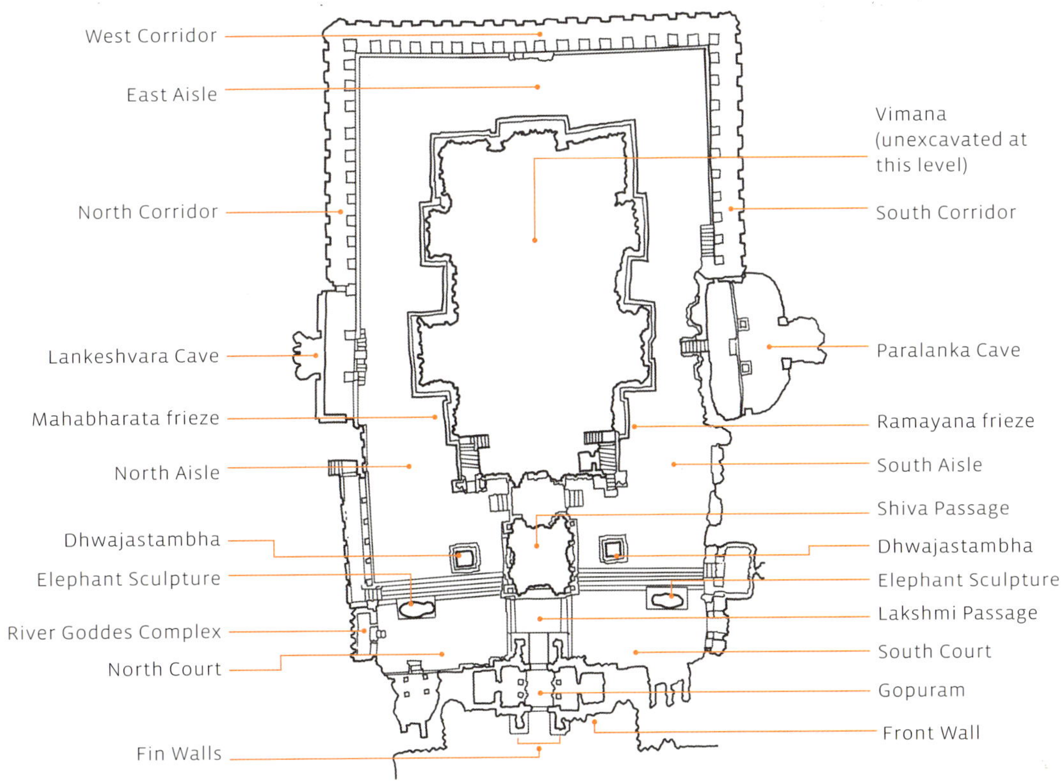

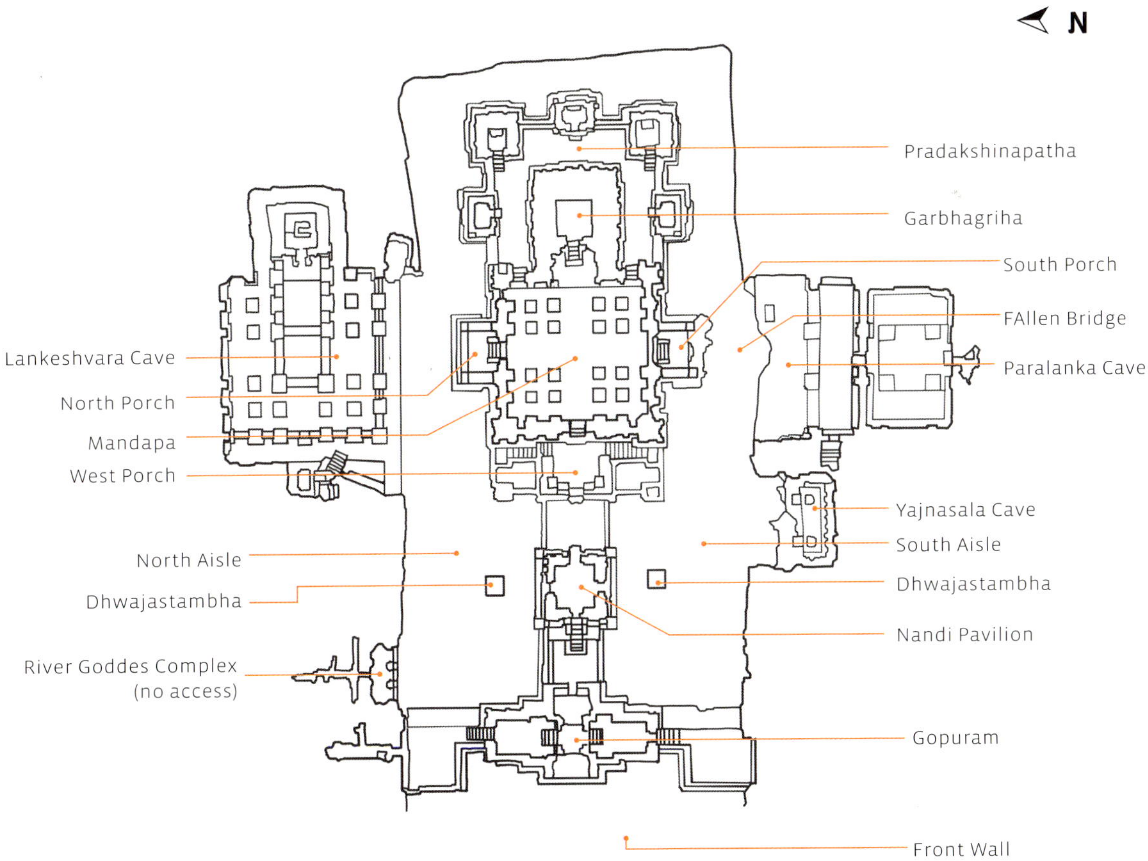

TOP
illustration A. Ground Floor Plan

ABOVE
illustration B. Upper Floor Plan

the Kailas. The wall's exterior is covered with sculptures of various gods, most now severely ravaged by centuries of dust storms and vandalism. A few remain in reasonable condition, however, such as the figures of Agni, god of fire astride his traditional 'vehicle' the goat, and Kartikeya, god of war, upon his peacock [figure 4].

It is possible before entering—indeed well worth the effort—to clamber up the rock ledges to the left of the wall, and make a complete circuit of the temple, enjoying dramatic close views of its *shikhara* [figure 5], roof sculptures, and a stunning panoramic view of the entire temple looking back toward its entrance from the highest point on its perimeter [see figure 1]. Illustrations of the Kailas in most books tend to be taken from points along this circuit. Enjoying these views is a vicarious experience, however: *looking* at it from the outside instead of *feeling* it from inside. The gut-level spatial impact of the Kailas is only to be experienced from within.

Passing through the *gopuram* we will explore, in sequence, the following spaces, each of which is shown on its appropriate floor plan: illustrations A (Ground Level) and B (Upper Level). At ground level is the Entrance Tunnel, leading through the *gopuram* to an entrance foyer (Lakshmi Passage), with its huge welcoming sculpture of that goddess. From here we will enter the North Court, with its River Goddess chapel, followed by the dramatic North Aisle beyond. Next we will climb up to the Lankeshvara Cave for its spectacular views of the *vimana*'s north face and the cave's magnificent sculpture of Shiva Nataraja; then return to the North Aisle and visit the Shiva Passage, the North, East and South Galleries, the Ravana Sculpture and the fallen bridge above it. After climbing to the mid-level of the Paralanka Cave for the extraordinary views it offers of the *vimana*'s south face, we will return to the South Aisle, take a side trip up to the Yajnasala Cave to view its powerful sculpture, and return through the South Court to the Lakshmi Passage. We will then climb to the Kailas's upper level via its North Stair to inspect the sculptures of the *vimana*'s West Porch, and visit the Nandi Pavilion, the temple's principal hall (*mandapa*), and the ambulatory *(pradakshinapatha)* encircling its *shikhara*. Finally we will enter its holiest place, the Kailas's womb-chamber, or *garbhagriha*.[1]

5. Shikhara, viewed from the north cliff

The Kailas incorporates dozens of deliberate design devices that guide its visitors on this metaphoric and spatial journey. These features are familiar to most architects, but rarely, if ever, noticed by lay observers (and surely not initiated by Krishnaraja). A powerful succession of them commences immediately as we step into the *gopuram*. Penetrating it at its base is a long, narrow, unlit Entrance Tunnel, lined with sculpted figures—barely discernable in the murky

6. First glimpse of Gajalakshmi sculpture, from Entrance Tunnel

blackness—that makes its way through the tower. The *gopuram* itself measures about twenty-five feet from front to back, but the Kailas's *sthapati* has artificially lengthened this passage to about forty feet by adding fin walls (identified on illustration A) on both its right and left sides, extending outward and inward from both the front and back of the tower.

Why, we may ask, did the *sthapati* do this?

Soundara Rajan, who is probably the only writer to take any notice of these fin walls, remarks that they are "apparently intended to enclose the [sculpted figures] within them."[2] A more likely explanation, however, would immediately spring to the mind of most architects. The Kailas's *sthapati* deliberately designed this space *not* as an art gallery, or as simply a way to move bodies from outside to inside, but as a *metaphoric passage*: one in which the visitor leaves behind the illusory world of mankind, and enters for the first time into the realm of God.

In his 2005 book *Concepts of Space in Traditional Indian Architecture,* architect Yatin Pandya has noted that Indian architecture has a long-standing tradition of leading visitors through its buildings from space to space by subtle modulations of room shape, height, scale, colour, textures, qualities of light and shade, variations in floor level, etc. "The journey in itself," he says, "becomes the event."[3] Nowhere is this more evident than in the design of the Kailas. The Entrance Tunnel is our first experience of this journey: a *designed* space in itself: dark, confining, mysterious. As we make our way through it a new vision looms ahead. Shining at its end is our first revelation of God's realm [figure 6]: a huge sculptural panel called Gajalakshmi (image of Lakshmi). At first only a slice of the panel itself can be made out, but as we draw nearer we see that it fills the far wall of a roofed foyer about twenty feet square, which I have called the Lakshmi Passage. The sculpture represents the welcoming Goddess Lakshmi, personification of beauty, prosperity, fertility and good fortune, seated upon a double lotus pad, and emerging at the dawn of creation from the primordial ocean, here represented in stone by a mass of lotus buds [figure 7].

7. Full view of Gajalakshmi sculpture

FACING PAGE

8. First view of the River Goddess Complex, viewed from Lakshmi Passage

Stepping into the foyer, we find ourselves in a space that has suddenly expanded left and right the entire 150 feet width of the Kailas's excavation. Its left and right sides are completely open to the sky and flooded with daylight, in stark contrast to the Entrance Tunnel's dark and narrow confinement. Why is this? Are these variances simply the accidental by-products of a random or thoughtless architectural process? Certainly they are not. The sudden openness and light that now enfolds us is a clear architectural statement that we have arrived in the domain of God.

(This abrupt release from darkness to light, and from confinement to expansiveness, is yet another welcoming device, familiar for centuries to architects of many cultures.)

Turning left for *pradakshina* (ritual circumambulation of the temple, always performed clockwise, keeping the venerated person or

object to the side of one's 'clean' right hand) we are confronted with our first view, framed by the inside face of the temple's massive front wall on our left and the Passage's ceiling above [figure 8], of one of the Kailas's most unforgettable visual revelations. Straight ahead, sixty feet away at the far end of a sunken courtyard, (the North Court), rises a towering rough-hewn cliff that is the north wall of the temple's excavation, gleaming in sudden full sunlight. At its base, but raised about six feet above the Court's floor, is a meticulously carved little cave, housing (although until the eye adjusts they cannot be made out in its dim interior) elegant over-life-size female figures, personifying three of India's great rivers: the Ganga (Ganges), Jamuna (Yamuna) and the mythical Sarasvati. Directly above, a matching cave is carved out of the cliff, its interior unfinished and inaccessible, and above this a vast, ominous pointed arch—struck from the cliff face, seemingly, by a few prodigious blows of some titanic hammer and chisel. (Or is it, perhaps, only a natural cleft of the primeval rock?) Together, these comprise the River Goddess Complex.

There is much for us to take in from this vantage point. First, there is the Courtyard itself. We must descend a few steps to enter it: indeed its floor is lower than any of the spaces that abut it. Why is this? As architects are well aware, it is an ingrained tendency within all of us as human beings to gravitate from darkness to light, and from higher to lower ground. Pandya remarks as well that the Courtyard has always been "a characteristic device of Indian architecture [creating] a world within a world...becoming a focus in itself."[4] By lowering its floor our *sthapati* has both clearly defined the boundaries of this space, and subtly invited us to enter the "world within a world" that now opens before us.

This space, the North Court, is bounded to our left by the inside surface of the Kailas's massive front wall, and to our right by two huge sculptural elements: an over-life-size elephant and a free-standing, fifty-foot stone obelisk, or banner stave (*dhwajastambha*),[5] close to the side of the *vimana* itself. (There is a matching South Court, a mirror image of the North Court, on the opposite side of the Lakshmi Passage, with its own elephant and *dhwajastambha*.) Both elephants and *stambhas* are carved from the pristine rock of the site, and thus are obviously part of the *sthapati*'s original intention. But what is their purpose, and why did he place them here?

Dhavalikar describes the carving on these *stambhas* in considerable detail, and quotes Brown that they are "in themselves finished works of art, gracefully proportioned yet strongly stable," adding, rather inscrutably, "their place in the architectural scheme being somewhat analogous to the obelisk in the Egyptian temple."[6] Soundara Rajan speculates that the *stambhas* are "employed to occupy the vacant open court and by their slenderness to furnish a measuring rod to the stature of the Kailasa Temple itself...a similar role is played by the two elephants facing inwards...Apparently the purpose of showing these elephants on the lower court a little to the rear of the flanks is to indicate in full form the popular motif of the Rashtrakuta [empire], namely, the elephants and to place them at the very entrance of their temple."[7]

While these erudite comments may enlighten us as to their physical detail, they miss the point of why the *sthapati* placed them there in the first place. A perceptive architect, however, would immediately understand that the *sthapati* deliberately positioned the North Court's elephant and *stambha* not to 'occupy' but to define the right hand boundary of the Courtyard itself—and to screen from the visitor (for the moment) the magnificent revelation of the North Aisle that awaits him just beyond. As for so much of the *sthapati*'s design conception, the human experiences of the Kailas are to be revealed one by one.

Second, from our vantage point we must digest the three-storied River Goddess Complex itself. Relatively few scholars have remarked on this complex, and those who have done so have dealt only with its individual parts. The middle cave in particular has been the subject of much debate because there is no access to it. In a 1952 journal article[8] art historian Hermann Goetz, taking note of this fact, and observing in addition that its front railing was notched in the middle down to its floor as if for a doorway [see figure 8], deduced that the ground level of this courtyard must therefore have been originally

9. The three River Goddesses: Sarasvati, Ganga and Jamuna, in the River Goddess chapel

planned at the floor level of the now-inaccessible cave, and have been subsequently excavated downward some twenty-five feet to its present location. Goetz knew that both elephants and *stambhas* were planned early on to stand in their present location (they are after all carved *in situ* from the virgin rock), but he argued, because of the middle cave's presumed doorway, that the Court's floor must have been planned even earlier to be at this upper 'doorway' level.

Goetz, however, failed to think through the architectural consequences of such a scenario. In the first place, the *dhwajastambha*, which must have been in place from top to bottom (since it was carved from the original rock of the site), would have projected a full twenty-five feet above his presumed upper floor. Perhaps it could have stood in a clumsy (and costly) pit or recess carved back into the elevated floor platform—but to what purpose? Providing ground-level access to this essentially useless little cave would have been at best a temporary measure, given that it had already been decided (as Goetz concedes) to excavate the courtyard downward to its present location within a relatively few years. In the second place, how would visitors entering the temple at the base of the *gopuram*, and emerging from its Entrance Tunnel in front of the Gajalakshmi sculpture have made their way up the twenty-five feet to Goetz's floor level? There is no indication that the temple's entrance might ever have been at the upper level of the *gopuram*: the window railing and massive lintel that are now there appear never to have been disturbed [see figure 3]. Therefore, if Goetz's theory were correct, there must have been stairs for this purpose within the North Court, and perhaps within the South Court as well. Given the need for a platform of reasonable width in front of the notch-fronted cave at the upper level, and the space required for the stairs themselves, the stairs and platform together would have essentially filled the entire Court. Turning left in front of the Gajalakshmi, the visitor would then have been immediately faced not with an open courtyard and a dramatic view of the cliff beyond (let alone of the River Goddess Complex itself), but a massive staircase starting almost immediately at the edge of the Lakshmi Passage. Lost also, in this scenario, would have been the powerful impact of spatial expansion, left and right, that we now feel on emerging from the Entrance

10. River Goddess Jamuna

Tunnel, the experience of major sculptures on the Court's walls, the River Goddess sculptures themselves, and the avenues for further exploration of the Temple's lower level to which the Court invites us—all of which are described below.

The impracticality of Goetz's contention was pointed out in 1968 by Stanislaw Czuma in his doctoral dissertation for the University of Michigan, and his conclusion was dispelled altogether (although without crediting Czuma for his effort) by Dhavalikar in his *Masterpieces of Rashtrakuta Art—The Kailas,* published in 1983. For three decades, however, Goetz's analysis held sway as the prevailing scholarly theory regarding the construction sequence of this portion of the Kailas.

If Goetz was wrong, then, how are we to explain the notched railing and the lack of access to the middle cave? First, we must recognize that the three components of the River Goddess Complex—the lower cave housing the sculptures, the inaccessible cave directly above and the great arch above that—are not individual, unrelated elements as scholars have generally regarded them, but together comprise a single visual conception. To see that this is so, one has only to place a finger over any one of these parts in figure 8, and observe how the visual impact of the entirety vanishes.

Had he wished to provide access to the upper cave, the Kailas's *sthapati* could easily have done so by adding just ten feet to the network of tunnels behind it, shown in the lower left corner of the Upper Level plan [see illustration B]. But suppose, in his conception, the function of the upper cave was purely visual. Looking again at figure 8, imagine for a moment a complex consisting only of the bottom cave, its interior defined by what appears as a black rectangle of empty space, the top of which is level with the elephant's eye. Above this rectangle imagine only bare cliff. The River Goddess Complex, thus reduced to this single cave, would clearly lack all of the visual impact that we see in it today. Now, however, insert the upper cave directly above it. The two caves together, visually linked by their vertically aligned central columns, now appear as a single space, their black interiors, now apparently separated from one another only by an intricately carved beam that spans between—and vanishes into—the rugged cliffs on both sides. And the 'doorway' notch in the railing? The downward-pointing stem of the upper cave's 'T'— shaped black mass now forms an essential visual tie to that of the lower cave, bringing their mysterious interiors together to be perceived as one contiguous space. Seen thus, the fact that the middle cave is inaccessible becomes totally irrelevant. Apart from the visual coherence of its tiered caves, the great dramatic arch that caps them, melting into its mountain before our very eyes as our ascending gaze reaches it, indelibly stamps this River Goddess Complex both as an immensely powerful artistic vision in its, own right, and as a grand metaphor of God's presence.

Advancing now to enter the lower cave, we may examine the three goddesses at close range [figure 9]. Ganga, representing purity, stands in the centre (as befits her status as the principal river), straight and upright upon her fantastic crocodile-like base, or *makara*. To her left and right respectively stand her sinuous tributaries, Jamuna [figure 10], representing devotion on her tortoise, and Sarasvati, the personification of knowledge, on a lotus pad. The elegant sculptures, although considerably weathered and vandalized, are among the finest in the temple. At one time (and perhaps, we might hope, once again in the future) the approach to them must have been even more spectacular, for as one ascends the short flight of stairs from the courtyard, a long depression in the cave's floor, six or eight inches deep, comes into view, stretching in front of the goddesses from left to right. Although no writer has probably remarked on it, this depression was no doubt once filled with water for symbolic ablution, as there is no other basin or 'tank' within the Kailas,—or even as a reflecting pool (another traditional Indian device cited by Pandya)—which would have produced a wonderful architectural effect.

Water, in Indian thought, is the ultimate source of all life. Lakshmi, as we saw moments ago on emerging from the Entrance Tunnel, was born of it when, according to myth, the gods and demons joined to churn the primordial ocean, releasing its blessings for the benefit of all mankind. Rivers are sacred as well, and none more so than the

Ganga. Prayag, (now Allahabad) is a *tirtha*, or holy crossing place, where the Ganga, Jamuna and (it is believed) the mythical Sarasvati rivers all flow together. Hundreds of thousands gather there every twelve years at a huge religious festival known as *Kumbha Mela* to wash away their sins. At Varanasi, the holiest place of all, every pilgrim's first obligation is a purifying bath in the Ganga's holy waters. Prayag and Varanasi, however, are hundreds of miles away to the north, and so their rivers are presented here in their symbolic form. Worshipping these three goddesses, according to M. N. Deshpande, is "like taking a spiritual bath in the *Prayagatirtha*, [so that one may] be endowed with purity and devotion, the prerequisites of knowledge"[9]—knowledge to be imparted, little by little, as the devotee pursues his journey into the mysteries of the Kailas.

Notes

1. Since no generally accepted names have been assigned, so far as I am aware, to the capitalized spaces in the foregoing paragraph, the designations I have given to them are my own.
2. Soundara Rajan, K. V. *The Ellora Monoliths*. Delhi: Gian, 1988, p. 90.
3. Pandya, Yatin. *Concepts of Space in Traditional Indian Architecture*. Ahmedabad: Mapin, 2005: pp. 14 & 20.
4. *Ibid.*, p. 20.
5. Fergusson, James. *History of Indian and Eastern Architecture*. 1876. Reprint, revised & edited by James Burgess, Delhi: Munshiram Manoharlal, 1967: p. 343
6. Brown, Percy. *Indian Architecture (Buddhist and Hindu Periods)*. Reprint, Bombay: Taraporevala, 1965: p. 74.
7. Soundara Rajan, K. V. *The Ellora Monoliths*. Delhi: Gian, 1988, p. 99.
8. Goetz, Hermann. "The Kailasa of Ellora and the Chronology of Rashtrakuta Art". In *Artibus Asiae* Vol. 15 Nos. 1 & 2 (1952).
9. Deshpande, M. N. "Kailasa: A Study in its Symbolism". In *Ellora Caves: Sculptures and Architecture*. Collected papers of the University Grants Commission's National Seminar. New Delhi: Books & Books, 1988, p. 243.

Yesterday and Today

As we emerge from the River Goddess Cave, a view opens across an as-yet unseen plaza, forty-five degrees left, framed by a column of the cave and the elephant's rump, of the entrance to a stair climbing to the main level of the *vimana* itself [figure 11] and the north *dhwajastambha* towering to the right. Ninety degrees to our left a passage opens leading directly to that great plaza, the North Aisle, staggeringly overhung by gigantic cliffs [figure 12]. We will explore both in due course. Tempting as they appear, however, let us first to examine in some depth a third vision. Directly across the Courtyard and just to the right of the Lakshmi Passage is one of the Kailas's major sculptures: a grand representation of the Goddess Durga slaying Mahishasura, the buffalo demon: the Devi-Mahishasuramardini (*Devi*=goddess, Mahisha=buffalo, *asura*=demon, *mardini*=killing) [figures 13 and 14]. The sculpture conveys in metaphor a message that remains vividly alive in the everyday life of Hindus today: one that sheds important insight onto the differences—and the striking similarities—between the Hinduism of today and that of thirteen centuries ago.

According to an ancient myth, the demon Mahishasura, after undergoing many penances in devotion to Brahma, was granted a boon by that god that he could never be killed by either god or man. Thus protected, he proceeded to subdue all the kings on earth, and then to overpower the gods themselves, expelling them from heaven. Even the great Shiva and Vishnu were powerless before him. However, unfortunately for him, his boon offered no protection against death at the hands of a woman. By pooling all of their energies, therefore, the gods created the terrible goddess Durga, who in a titanic battle ultimately slew the demon, restoring order to the world.

At the bottom of this panel we see Durga, 'side-saddle' on her lion mount as he surges toward the great *asura*, trampling his minions underfoot. From her upraised bow she has just released three arrows, seen speeding toward the demon's head. With each of her ten arms bearing a weapon given to her by one of the gods, she prepares to deliver the death blow to Mahishasura, represented here with a human head and body (the former bearing buffalo horns), wielding a huge club. Above, a host of the gods witness the scene with satisfaction.

A straightforward tale of Good triumphant over Evil? It is far more than that.

Unable to defeat the great Mahishasura themselves, the gods, by creating the fearsome Durga,

> in a gesture of perfect surrender and fully willed self abdication... returned their energies to the primeval *Shakti*, the One Force, the fountain head, whence originally all had stemmed...Life Energy itself as the primeval maternal principle, had reabsorbed them, eaten them back into the universal womb.[1]

LEFT

11. Visitors enter the North Stair, looking southeast from the steps of the River Goddess Complex

RIGHT

12. North Aisle, looking east from the River Goddess Complex steps

13. Mahishasuramardini sculpture, looking south from River Goddess Complex

FACING PAGE

14. Mahishasurmardini sculpture (other view)

Devi, the Great Mother, is among the most compelling and widely venerated figures in the Hindu pantheon. Undoubtedly one of the most ancient, pre-Aryan deities of India, she is sometimes presented as a beautiful blooming woman, sometimes as a frightening slut. All the characteristic qualities of the original mother-deity are concentrated in her: femininity and fertility as well as destructive violence, charm as well as terrifying cruelty. She is the embodiment of *Shakti*, the divine female creative power.[2]

The powerful figure of the family matriarch is readily identified within the subconscious of Hindus today—men and women alike—

with that of Devi, the Great Mother of ancient myth. Even today, most Hindu marriages in India are still arranged by the bride's and groom's parents. The couple themselves may never even have met beforehand. Immediately after the wedding the bride is delivered to the household of the groom's joint family—often accompanied by a substantial dowry—perhaps far away from her home and from everyone she has ever known. There she falls under the absolute domination of its unquestioned mistress, her new mother-in-law, and there she remains, a virtual servant—until she bears a son. The son is her saviour, a young god, heaven-sent to deliver her from her private hell, and it is as a god that he is treated. He responds in kind. An intense bond of mutual dependency develops between mother and son, often lasting a lifetime. The final act of the drama is played out when the son himself marries, and his mother becomes the mistress of *his* household.

What is the emotional impact of this cycle on the Hindu son? Sudhir Kakar, perhaps India's leading contemporary psychiatrist, offers some insight, relating yet another version of the Devi-Mahishasuramardini story:

> The demon Mahishasura had conquered all the three worlds. Falling in love with the goddess, he sent a message to make his desire known to her. Devi replied that she would accept as her husband only someone who defeated her in battle. Mahishasura entered the battlefield with a vast army and a huge quantity of equipment. Devi came alone mounted on her lion, without even armor, riding naked to the combat. Dismounting, Devi started dancing and cutting off the heads of millions and millions of demons with her sword to the rhythm of her movement. Mahishasura, facing death, tried to run away by becoming an elephant. Devi cut off his trunk. The elephant became a buffalo and against its thick hide Devi's sword and spear were of no avail. Angered, Devi jumped on the buffalo's back and rode it to exhaustion. When the buffalo demon's power of resistance had collapsed, Devi plunged her spear into its ear and Mahishasura fell dead [figure 15].

15. Durga slaying Mahishasura, Ellora Cave no. 17

"The myth is stark enough in its immediacy," Kakar adds, "and needs no more gloss on the omnipotence and sexual energy of the goddess, expressed in the imagery of her dancing and riding naked, exhausting even the most powerful male to abject submission and death, [and] decapitating (i.e. castrating) millions of 'bad boys' with demonic desires."

Perceiving this same omnipotence and energy in his own mother and seeing these images "perpetuated through Hindu myths, folk beliefs, proverbs, symbols, and the ritual worship of the goddess in her terrible and fierce forms," the Hindu son feels "hopelessly inadequate in the face of her imagined sexual overpoweringness," and is beset with "fears of being engulfed and swallowed by her dark depths." He experiences guilt-ridden fears of castration and lurking desires to be female. Deep-seated "fear and dread pervades men's fantasies of women," while in response "anger and disappointment are a large part of the women's feelings in relationship to men... Cultural ideas and ideals of masculinity and femininity, then, manifested in their narrative forms as myths, pervade the innermost experiences of the self."[3]

The Devi-Mahishasuramardini is thus an over-arching metaphor for the eternal conflict between Man and Woman that has characterized every civilization since the dawn of history. Devi, beautiful, desirable, cruel, unattainable, all-powerful, represents every woman; Mahishasura, strong, courageous, heroic, but in the end fatally vulnerable, represents every man. The myth, like the conflict it symbolizes, remains vibrantly alive today in the Hindu psyche. The drama is played out all over India every October in immensely popular Navratri ('Nine Nights') festivals, in which huge images of both Devi and Mahishasura are paraded and worshipped for nine nights by throngs of millions, and concludes on the tenth with re-enactment of their final battle, and its inevitable outcome. Yet this is not The End—for in Hindu thought every death is inevitably followed by rebirth. The myth, and Mahishasura's death within it, remain unreal, for, as Rowland has aptly put it: "In Indian art, as in Indian philosophy, all life, even that of the gods, is a *lila*, an illusion or play set against the background of eternity."[4] Within the Kailas this

16. 'God is present everywhere': Nandi gaurding the Shiva linga

background, quite literally, is its omnipresent enclosure of towering rough-hewn cliffs: themselves a gigantic, deliberate metaphor bespeaking the presence of God.

The Devi-Mahishasuramardini story is a striking example of how an ancient myth has remained a living presence in the everyday lives of Hindus, from the time the Kailas was carved—and long before—to the present day. Hundreds of other tales have done so as well, and we will examine several as we make our way through the Kailas. Many are contemporary with the creation of the Kailas, and thus, like the temple itself, are products of (or perhaps an impetus for) Hinduism's great popular surge in the middle centuries of that millennium, in which it overwhelmed Buddhism to become the dominant religion of India that it is today.

This surge coincided with the rise of a Hindu movement known as *bhakti* ('devotion'), in which the worshipper establishes direct one-on-one contact with the deity, who takes residence in an object for this purpose. Their relationship is one of mutual love, and total submission of the devotee to the deity. The object in which the god is present may be a sculptural image, an aniconic image such as (in the case of Shiva) a *lingam* [figure 16], or simply a shrub or a stone with a few daubs of paint on it. It doesn't matter: God is present everywhere. Usually the contact takes place through the eyes, as *darshan*, "the act of seeing with complete understanding of the thing seen,"[5] as Kramrisch puts it (for India is an intensely visual land). *Bhakti* and *darshan*, contrasting so dramatically with the esoteric rituals of Vedic priests and Buddhist monks who had formerly dominated religious practice, quickly gained enormous popularity among the people at large. Moreover, the new fervour was accompanied by tremendous new vitality in the visual arts, producing in the sixth, seventh and eighth centuries much of India's greatest sculpture, as many of the ancient myths, revived in India's two great epics—the *Ramayana* and the *Mahabharata*, and in the *Puranas* (Stories of Old), were presented in vibrant forms never seen before.

Nowhere was this revolutionary spirit more apparent than in the Kailas. Yet there is scant written record of either the Kailas's creation or of its original religious activity. Other than the Baroda Grant, only one of the dozens of these contemporary documents unearthed so far is believed to refer to the building. This is the Kadoba Grant, an inscription on copper sheets dated 813 CE, the primary purpose of which was to confirm the grant of the village of Jalamangala to a temple in the city of Manayapura (possibly present-day Malkhed, near Gulbarga). It also contains a brief history of numerous Rashtrakuta kings (each, if the text is to be believed, a paragon of virtue), and the following description of a temple called Kannesvara, which the Grant's translator claims to be the Kailas:

> This excellent temple...seemed to have been created during hundreds of *Kritayugas* (cyclical ages of time that repeat one another *ad infinitum*. Each *Kritayuga* is said to equal 1,728,000 years). The clouds, their masses increasing by the smoke of the burnt *aloo* [potato] incense, and their summits being mounted to the Siddhis [supernatural powers] besprinkle its court with their pure, fragrant waters...When at night the blazing lamps have been fixed on the outsides of the pinnacles and battlements[6] that touch the groups of the stars, the division of the night is in good disorder, the citizens thinking that the morning has come...[This

> temple] which, covered with thousands of colored banners, shone honored, as it were through devotion to Parameshvara [supreme overlord], by the one-crest jewel of the world [the sun, that] out of fear of moving above had descended of its own accord in the guise of its image that was reflected in the jewel-paved [i.e. by reflected sunlight] floor; where the peacocks, their passion being raised by hearing the deep sounds of the beaten drums, commenced to perform their dances, as if the beginning of the rainy season had caused their exaltation; where minds of the citizens' young women were enchanted by the dances of moon-faced girls that were skilled in manifesting by [the gestures of] their sprout-like hands the true state of sentiments and affections of lovely maidens engaged in wanton sport at the time of smoke [of evening fires rising?] which was filled by hundreds of sages who had crossed the ocean of all Siddhautas [Saints]... which bears the name of Kanneshvara.[7]

This text certainly presents a vibrant and colourful picture of life in and around the temple in its early years: indeed a carnival atmosphere, with throngs of people of all ages filling it night and day, blazing lamps everywhere, billowing smoke and incense, thousands of coloured banners, courts besprinkled with pure scented water, lovely maidens engaged in wanton sport, enchanting moon-faced dancing girls and peacocks, deep-sounding drums, hundreds of sages from afar. A far cry indeed from the behaviour that adherents of many other faiths would consider appropriate within their places of worship. Life at the Kailas is certainly quieter now—but the spirit of those early days may not yet have entirely disappeared. During my last visit a rollicking game of *phugdi*, (in which the players pair off, hold hands and twirl each other about, to see who will be the last one standing) broke out among a sizable group of sari-clad women [figure 17] in the South Aisle just a few steps from the Ravana sculpture, attracting an enthusiastic audience of cheering spectators. The game has been handed down from mother to daughter over countless generations—perhaps even dating back to the time of the Kadoba Grant!

Hindu beliefs and practices of today are in any event firmly rooted in millennia of history. Dancing girls are no longer to be seen in

17. Women play the game of *phugdi* in South Aisle

FACING PAGE
18. Nandi with attendant, Virupaksha Temple, Pattadakal

Hindu temples, although dance performances derived from ancient religious models are an active art form, and there are temples where monkeys, snakes and rats are still worshipped. Oil lamps, banners, smoke, bells, drums, chanting, burning incense, colour, garlands of fresh flowers, purifying water, and hundreds of pairs of bare feet treading hot stone pavements, crowding forward for fleeting *darshan* of the *lingam* in a womb-chamber, as at the Kailas thirteen hundred years ago, are to be seen in hundreds of temples throughout India today [figure 18] "Hinduism today," says Philip Ashby, "is an integrated body of beliefs and actions that serve not as possible keys to a proper understanding of the human situation, but rather *the* correct beliefs and *the* appropriate conduct made absolutely imperative because these beliefs are internalized as life-sustaining verities."[8]

From the Kadoba Grant we can also conclude that many of the Kailas's sculptures, now hidden in dark corners, were once dramatically lit with torches, giving the *vimana* and its lateral caves carved from the surrounding cliffs an entirely different appearance from that which we see today. The temple is now closed at night, but many of its sculptures are located in recesses that receive virtually no light even on bright sunny days. In all probability, flickering torches were deliberately used to instil a quality of mystery and surprise to many of these subjects. We can now only imagine their impact—and perhaps, in our mind's eye, conjure up a vision of their effect, as I have suggested that we do here and there as we move through the temple. It is of course out of the question to re-install oil-burning torches here because of the smoke damage that would result, but perhaps some imaginatively designed electric illumination might one day be brought in. This has been attempted to a considerable extent—though with limited success in my view—at the nearby cave site of Ajanta.

Notes

1. Zimmer, Heinrich. *Myths and Symbols in Indian Art and Civilization*, ed. Joseph Campbell. 1946. Reprint: Princeton University Press, 1972, p. 12.
2. Mode, Heinz. *The Woman in Indian Art*. New York: McGraw Hill, 1970, p. 12.
3. This and the previous several quotes in the two preceding paragraphs are from Kakar, Sudhir. *Intimate Relations: Exploring Indian Sexuality*. University of Chicago Press, 1989, p. 138, but are presented here in a slightly different sequence.
4. Rowland, Benjamin. *The Art & Architecture of India: Buddhist/Hindu/Jain*. Baltimore: Penguin, 1967, p. 190.
5. Kramrisch, Stella. *The Hindu Temple*. 1946. Reprint, Delhi: Motilal Banarsidass, 1976, p. 38.
6. This suggests that the Kadoba Grant indeed refers to the Kailas, as the top of its front wall is 'battlemented' with recesses as if for gun ports.
7. H. Lüders, in *Epigraphica Indica*, Vol. IV, pp. 334-37 (1882).
8. Ashby, Philip H. *Modern Trends in Hinduism*. New York: Columbia University Press, 1960, p. 48 (emphasis his).

Akasha

Resuming our journey through the Kailas, we now pass from the North Court into the vast chasm between the *vimana* and the excavation's overpowering north face: the North Aisle. Either the forty-five degree route [see figure 11] or the ninety degree one [see figure 12] from the River Goddess chapel will lead us here, but perhaps the latter is the more dramatic. The North Aisle, its proportions long, narrow and strongly vertical, is yet another clearly delimited and powerfully designed *space*. Advancing into it, we are dwarfed—intimidated—*overwhelmed* by gigantic, jagged, ominously projecting masses of raw rock that soar upward over our left shoulder. The upward sweeping, elegantly carved spire of the *vimana* ascends skyward to our right. Straight ahead, in the distance, puny figures are illuminated in a slender shaft of sunlight [figure 19]—silhouetted against the impenetrable blackness beneath the east cliff's gravity-defying face, projecting as it does a full thirty feet from the solid mountain wall behind. The North Aisle is India's—if not the world's—ultimate architectural expression of *akasha*.

Akasha, signifying space, or ether, is regarded in Hindu thought as the foremost of the five elements that comprise the universe, the others being, in increasing degree of condensation, air, fire, water and earth. According to Stella Kramrisch, *akasha* is "the element which corresponds to *Prakriti*, the primordial substance, out of which evolves all that is manifest. Ether fills everything, it is all pervading. It is in the air and it is in the stone."[1] "The relationship of solid and void in Indian sculpture," writes the sculptor Carmel Berkson, "symbolizes the endless proliferation of the world manifested, as all forms of the temporal world are linked to one another in complex profusion of associated volume and space...the voids *are* the sculpture as well."[2] (Similar views have been expressed by other sculptors of our time, notably Henry Moore and Barbara Hepworth.) Here, in the Kailas's North Aisle, the great void that fills it *is* the architecture—the deliberate, purposeful creation of a human mind—as well. Yet the words '*akasha*' or 'ether' or even 'space' rarely appear in scholarly commentary regarding the Kailas in any context, let alone as fully intended conceptions of its *sthapati*.

19. North Aisle, looking east

Unseen, unmentioned, *space* virtually does not exist in the work of Fergusson, Burgess, Brown, Dhavalikar, Soundara Rajan, and many others. It is nevertheless a real and powerful component not only of architecture, but of our everyday human experience as well. It is a rare person indeed who can remain unmoved by it standing on the rim of Arizona's Grand Canyon, even though the space that unfolds before him cannot be 'seen'. We do not have to travel to such a dramatic spot as this to experience it, however, for it is everywhere around us: as we pass from a narrow street into the openness of a city square, or when sunshine magically explodes on our landscape after a sudden summer shower, or when within an ordinary building we simply move from a low-ceilinged area to a high one. Or when, as we have seen, we suddenly emerge from a dark entrance tunnel into a brightly lit Lakshmi Passage. Yet perceiving—*feeling*—this impact is an ability that most of us habitually and unconsciously suppress. In doing so—by shutting off the faucet of our senses—we cheat ourselves every day of marvellous journeys of the spirit. The spatial experience of the Kailas is among the greatest of these journeys that the world of architecture has to offer. It is available to whomever among us are willing to open the faucet and let the awareness of our senses flow.

Although the North Aisle may present the Kailas's single most dramatic and powerful image of *akasha,* this temple abounds in experiences of it, in settings both violent and serene, terrifying and sublime. We shall see more examples of all of these in the pages that follow, beginning with an essential side trip up to the Lankeshvara Cave, hewn deep into the north cliff face directly above.

To our left as we pass into the North Aisle, a flight of steps (just behind the woman in a red shawl in figure 12) climbs to a short colonnaded passage. Following it to the right, we come face to face at its end with a carved Gajalakshmi, a smaller version of the panel that greeted us as we emerged from the Entrance Tunnel. To its left a rude stone stair vanishes upward into total blackness [figure 20]. We grope our way up, perceiving that it veers sharply right after rising twelve or fifteen feet: a few rays of daylight grudgingly illuminate the final ascent. No decoration embellishes this roughly cut, twisting, slanting tunnel;

20. Stair to Lankeshvara Cave, with second Gajalakshmi sculpture at its base

even the flickering flame of some ancient torch could not have relieved the potent sense of awe that it evokes. Burgess complains that it is "badly lit."[3] Czuma and others have speculated that it was intended only as a temporary access route, to be replaced with a grander one in a different location, perhaps from deep within the unfinished lower storey of the Lankeshvara Cave. However, I doubt this was ever intended, for the present stair is entirely consistent, Burgess's criticism notwithstanding, with the aura of mystery to be found throughout the Kailas. Here, as at the Entrance Tunnel, and indeed at every other transitional space throughout the temple, its *sthapati* has given us—quite deliberately—no hint as we enter of what will be revealed at its end. Our passage through each of these is a metaphoric journey: through the darkness of ignorance to the light of divine revelation.

We emerge from the stair into a corridor along the west wall of the Lankeshvara Cave. Here we must turn left or right, as our way straight ahead is barred by a waist-high stone wall, separating the corridor from the cave's main space. To our left, the corridor extends deep into the cliff: huge sculptures are barely visible in the depths of the Lankeshvara Cave's murky interior. To our right, however, yet another experience of space pulls us irresistibly toward it. There, directly in front of us and at the same level at which we now stand, lies the West Porch of the *vimana* itself, bathed in the daylight of which we have just been so utterly deprived [figure 21].

As we are drawn toward this vision we are immediately distracted by a long view to our left, across the wall, to a stunning image of Shiva dancing the *tandava* [figure 22]—but investigation of it must wait: the draw of the *vimana* ahead is too great to resist. Continuing toward it, our corridor ends at a long open terrace stretching the full width of the cave along its cliff edge. Only a twenty-five feet deep chasm—the North Aisle, now viewed from above—separates this terrace from the *vimana,* looming across the chasm a mere twenty feet away, seemingly close enough to reach out and touch. Our view of the *vimana* expands at every step: the entire south front of our cave, like the wide-angle lens of a colossal camera, has seemingly opened wide before our eyes, focusing entirely on the *vimana*'s West Porch, alive

21. First glimpse of Vimana's West Porch, looking south from Lankeshvara west corridor

22. First glimpse of Shiva Nataraja sculpture in Lankeshvara Cave, viewed from west corridor

with a constant stream of colourfully clad visitors, emerging from the temple's entrance stairs and disappearing into its *mandapa*, or great hall [figure 23]. A massive ceiling of living rock projects out above our head; ceiling, floor and side walls, like huge sun baffles, combine to enclose this scene within the raw stone edges of our imaginary camera's powerful visual frame.

As we move outward toward the terrace's edge, a superb panorama opens up magically before us. Deep below lies the floor of the North Aisle, where we stood in awe moments before. Far to our right rises the *gopuram*; to the left of it our eye moves past the North *Stambha* and Nandi Pavilion to the West Porch. Next the North Porch comes into view, flanked by its splendid sculptures. Still farther left the great *shikhara*, Shiva's mountain itself, soars upward above its *garbhagriha*. Finally, to our extreme left, we see the inner *pradakshinapatha*, the ambulatory that encircles this holiest place, its five subsidiary shrines—each a replica in miniature of the principal *shikhara* itself—splayed against the sky and vast sunlit cliffs: a constant reminder that we are here within God's domain.

From the River Goddess Complex the Kailas's *sthapati* has led us, subtly but surely, into the North Aisle to experience its grandeur from below. Then, in a deliberately planned sequence of spatial experiences, he has led us through a cathartic black stairway to a revelatory, sunlit vision of the same space from an entirely different perspective. What he has designed for us here is not the Lankeshvara Cave's stone, but its invisible space—its *akasha*: "*Prakriti*, the primordial substance, out of which evolves all that is manifest."

Let us take a moment to reflect on how he accomplished this.

In plan (that is, in its horizontal dimensions), the Lankeshvara Cave is a rectangle, approximately ninety feet wide by eighty feet deep, carved straight back into the temple's north cliff. Its side and rear walls are thus windowless. Its front face is parallel and completely open to the North Aisle, terminating in a terrace that stretches along the cliff's edge for the cave's entire width. The terrace is consequently brilliantly illuminated by sunlight, while the cave's

23. Vimana's West Porch, viewed from Lankeshvara terrace

low-ceilinged interior quickly becomes pitch dark as one moves back into it, even on the sunniest days. The column layout of the Lankeshvara Cave's main space is almost identical to that of the *vimana*'s principal *mandapa*, or great hall. Spatially, however, as a comparison of figures 22 and 58 will instantly reveal, the two are at opposite poles. The Lankeshvara Cave's ceiling height is roughly half that of the *vimana*'s, giving it a strongly horizontal character, in contrast with its counterpart's powerfully vertical one—an effect vividly reinforced by the conspicuous horizontal striations on Lankeshvara Cave's ceiling and its horizontally elongated column capitals, plainly visible in figure 22. Burgess presents his view of cave architecture in general, and of the design of the Lankeshvara Cave in particular, as follows:

> Like all rock-cut examples...the caves have the intolerable defect of having no exterior form. The only parts of them which strictly belong to architectural art are their pillars...such a pillar as this one [here he illustrates their stubby appearance with his own drawing of a square pillar with a shaft height to width ratio of approximately 1.3 to 1] from the cave called Lankeshvara on the side of the pit in which the Kailas stands. Though in exquisite taste as a rock-cut example, where the utmost strength is apparently required to support the mass of rock above, [it] does not afford any points of comparison with structural examples of the same age. In a building it would be cumbersome and absurd; under a mass of rock it is elegant and appropriate.[4]

The Lankeshvara Cave's pillars are indeed elegant and appropriate to their setting. All of the columns in this cave are exquisitely carved. Burgess may also be correct that their squat proportions are necessary from a structural point of view (although there are other locations within the Kailas where comparable loads are successfully supported by taller, slenderer and more widely spaced columns.) However, his assertion that the caves' lack of external form constitutes an "intolerable defect" and that only their pillars belong to architectural art, plus his implication that the Kailas itself consists only of the *vimana* within the "pit," all reflect the pervasive scholarly mindset that sees only its stones, and remains blind to its *akasha*, its metaphor—and to the *architectural intent* of the *sthapati* who designed this cave.

Architecture is not so simple an activity that *any* design choice can be reduced to a single motivation. I suggest, however, that the Lankeshvara Cave was in large part conceived and designed as a *theatre* from which to view the *vimana*. The entire cave focuses on it. It does so by its progression from the blackness of its interior to the explosion of light at its terrace, inviting us to move instinctively toward the light. It does so by its low ceiling height, terminating in a huge projecting roof slab over the terrace, in effect creating (spatially) a strong horizontal thrust of the entire cave outward toward the terrace and *vimana*. (Has no one ever wondered *why* this ceiling was designed so much lower than any other in the temple?)

It does so by framing—horizontally and vertically—the constantly expanding view it offers of the *vimana* as one approaches it step by step. It even did so, originally at least, by avoiding any visual barrier at the outer edge of the terrace—for there was apparently no guardrail there until the Archaeological Survey of India (ASI)[5] installed one in recent years.

This terrace offers us what is effectively our first view of the *vimana*—for it cannot be visually comprehended from below—and this terrace offers by far the most spectacular vision of it from anywhere within the temple. It is a panorama that widens before our eyes as we

24. Vimana's West Porch, viewed from Lankeshvara terrace, now fenced off

advance toward it, ultimately expanding to reveal the Kailas's entire free-standing central *vimana*, from *gopuram* to our extreme right to the *shikhara* and the east cliff face far to our left. We are led to the terrace as we emerge from the stair by the wall or the railing in front of us, and by the sudden transition from the darkness of the stair itself to the brilliantly illuminated terrace to our right. Our aisle, as we approach the terrace, is directly aligned with, and at exactly the same level as the *vimana*'s main arrival point, its West Porch.

None of this is random or accidental. It is a sequence of spatial experiences deliberately planned by the Kailas's *sthapati*. And

25. Shiva Nataraja sculpture, Lankeshvara Cave

no architect would argue that his effort failed to qualify as "architectural art."

The preceding twelve paragraphs were written in 2009, and accurately reflected the conditions and the human impact of the Lankeshvara Cave at that time. In 2012, however, the ASI had installed a wall-to-wall, floor-to-

ceiling wire mesh fence along the inner edge of the cave's terrace [figure 24], completely blocking all access to the terrace itself, confining its visitors behind a prison-like metal barrier, and effectively cancelling out the superb panoramic views it had offered of the entire vimana. *The stated purpose of this barrier is to keep bats from roosting in the dark interior of the cave.*

It might be pointed out that this was apparently the first time in the Lankeshvara Cave's thirteen-and-a-half centuries of existence that measures were considered necessary to keep the bats out. Are they really necessary today? One might also wonder, if indeed they are, if less drastic measures might have been tried first. Bat Conservation International, *for instance, offers guidelines for bat exclusion employing light-weight, flexible plastic netting hanging loose over roosting areas.*

At this point, however, the possibility of persuading ASI to consider any such alternatives is surely remote.

There is an important parallel to be drawn, however, between the administrative mindset that underlies this 'solution' to the bat problem and the detail-oriented academic mindset that pervades much of the Kailas scholarship. All too often these scholars—and the ASI as well—intent on examining each issue they address in detail or in isolation, fail to see them in their larger context. ASI, focused perhaps on preserving from damage some of the sculptures in the dark recesses of the Lankeshvara Cave, may have solved that problem, but in the course of doing so has blinded itself to the devastating spatial impact this effort has had on the terrace. Space in Hindu thought, according to Stella Kramrisch, is ("all pervading: it is in the air and in the stone,")— but concern for it is not to be found in ASI's approach to bat control.

*Throughout this text I have pointed out the near-universal absence of any reference to space in the work of many prominent Kailas scholars, and have identified many errors resulting from these omissions. The design of the Kailas can only be truly understood through comprehension not only of its physical forms, but also of the invisible, yet ever-present space—*akasha*—that envelops them all.*

There remains one sculpture here in the Lankeshvara Cave to be marvelled at in the light of day. It is Shiva dancing the furious *tandava* [figure 25], first glimpsed in the distance, in an extraordinary vision of space, as we moved to the terrace from the top of the stair [see figure 22]. Cruelly vandalized as it is, this is one of the most powerful images of Shiva within the Kailas, and perhaps in all of Indian art. The god's left leg is missing (although its foot can still be seen below), as are one of his left and two of his right arms. Yet his torso, elegantly curved in the *tribhanga* (triple bend) pose, surges from the wall behind it and virtually pulsates with wild energy—while Shiva's face maintains an aspect of perfect calm. This is the metaphor of the *tandava*: wild energy, the frenetic passage of human life from birth to death and the sublime calm of the Absolute come together here in the single form of Shiva. They are inseparable parts of a single Reality: they are one and the same. In the Hindu view of life, all phenomena are merely aspects of a single whole: a single reality: a single Absolute. Save for this sole reality, everything is *maya*, transient, in constant change.

Shiva's gestures, writes Heinrich Zimmer,

> wild and full of grace, precipitate the cosmic illusion; his flying arms and legs and the swaying of his torso produce—indeed, they are—the continuous creation/destruction of the universe, death exactly balancing birth, annihilation the end of every coming forth...We and the Divine are one and the same, precisely as the vitality of these swaying limbs is one and the same with the utter unconcern of the Dancer who flings them into play.[6]

In what is sometimes referred to (loosely) as the Hindu Trinity, Brahma is said to be the Creator, Vishnu the Preserver, and Shiva the Destroyer. The *tandava* is a fearsome dance of destruction that

Shiva is said to perform as "the demon of the cemetery" on dark and stormy nights in cremation grounds. "Shiva is a destroyer and loves the burning ground.[7] But what is it that Shiva destroys," asks Ananda Coomaraswamy, "in his role as Shri Nataraja, Lord of the Dance?" Once again the answer is to be found in metaphor. It is

> not merely the heavens and earth at the close of a world cycle, but the fetters that bind each separate soul. Where and what is the burning ground? It is not the place where our earthly bodies are cremated, but the hearts of His lovers, laid waste and desolate. The place where the ego is destroyed signifies the state where illusion and deeds are burnt away: *that* is the crematorium, the burning-ground where Shri Nataraja dances, and whence he is named *Sudalaiyadi*, Dancer of the burning-ground.[8]

Seen in Western terms, the *tandava* may seem horrifying and macabre, and its dancer the heartless soul of evil. But as interpreted through Hindu conceptions of death and reality, it is very different indeed. To a believer, the *tandava* is a metaphoric expression of profound truth, offering enlightenment and ultimate hope to mankind. Coomaraswamy affirms this view simply, by quoting a Bengali hymn to the Goddess Kali, Shiva's female aspect, "for whose entrance the heart must be purified by fire, made empty by redemption:"

> *Because Thou lovest the Burning-ground,*
> *I have made a Burning-ground of my heart —*
> *That Thou, Dark One, haunter of the Burning-ground*
> *Mayest dance Thy eternal dance.*
> *Naught else is within my heart, O Mother:*
> *Day and night blazes the funeral pyre:*
> *The ashes of the dead, strewn all about,*
> *I have preserved against Thy coming.*
> *With death-conquering Mahakala*[9] *'neath Thy feet*
> *Do Thou enter in, dancing Thy rhythmic dance,*
> *That I may behold Thee with closed eyes.*[10]

Before leaving the Lankeshvara Cave, I would like to examine a theory propounded by Hermann Goetz that relates to it tangentially.

26. Shiva Nataraja, north face of Nandi Pavilion basement

Until at least the tenth century, he argued, the floor of the North Aisle in front of the Lankeshvara Cave had not been excavated down to its present location, but only to the level of the Lankeshvara Cave's floor, twenty-five feet higher than the aisle is today. Goetz argued that this would have explained the presence of the Lankeshvara Cave's balcony terrace—for in his scenario it would originally have been not a balcony at all, but simply a level passage, directly linking the cave and the *vimana* at the same level. This theory, however, ignores a number of significant factors. The first of these is the presence of the main temple's North Porch, which projects into the North Aisle directly opposite the Lankeshvara Cave's 'terrace', and which virtually all scholars believe to have been carved (along with the rest of the *vimana*) in the mid-eighth century. The floor of this porch is at the same level as the terrace. Access to it from Goetz's elevated North Aisle, however, would have been completely blocked by the waist-high stone walls that enclose it on its three open sides.

27. Shiva Mahayogi sculpture, east wall of the Shiva Passage

Thus it would have sat like an enormous bathtub, inaccessible, on top of Goetz's Aisle for—according to his chronology—more than two hundred years.

Second, the position of the L-shaped railing or wall inside the Lankeshvara Cave itself would have made little sense, squeezing visitors entering the cave from the North Aisle into a narrow corridor along its left-hand wall, while barring them from direct access to the sanctuary straight ahead. The configuration of this corridor and the waist-high wall alongside it make much more sense as architectural elements guiding visitors from the stair to the terrace, as described above, than as an entrance to the cave from an elevated North Aisle.

Third, and perhaps most importantly, Goetz's theory does not reflect a serious understanding of the hugely detrimental architectural impact it would have had on the North Court (in front of the River

BELOW

28. Shiva Bhairava, west wall of the Shiva Passage

RIGHT

29. Shiva Bhairava (detail of figure 28)

Goddess Complex), and on the portion of the North Aisle between this Court and the "point near the present stair to the *vimana*," where he claimed its floor level jumped up to that of the Lankeshvara Cave. Goetz argued that both of these spaces, North Aisle and North Court, in fact comprised a single space: a single courtyard. Goetz's 'courtyard' would thus have been a split-level space (for the North Aisle's floor is half a dozen steps higher than the present North Court), and would have been divided into two parts by the *dhwajastambha* and elephant standing in the middle of it.

Such a space, however, would not have constituted a 'courtyard' at all within the context of Hindu thought—or for that matter within the context of Western (or Chinese, or Japanese) thought either. A courtyard, in all of these cultures, is a space of arrival and repose; a space in which to pause, not to rush through. It is a space for contemplation; a self-contained environment of inherent unity, the boundaries of which are clearly perceptible. Goetz's 'courtyard' would have displayed none of these qualities. Divided in two by a flight of steps, a huge *dhwajastambha*, and a gigantic elephant,

30. Shiva Mahayogi (detail of figure 27)

it would no longer have been perceivable as a single environment. From no point within it could all of its boundaries have been seen. It would have lacked any sense of arrival, or repose, or unity, or self-containment.

"The Indian notion of existence," writes Yatin Pandya, "rests on dualities: *Atman*, the infinitesimal building blocks of the human spirit, and *Brahman*, the overall schema of the universe, are the fundamental basis of any existence. This schema of dual existence simultaneously accepts the part as a whole and the whole as a part, and gives rise to the concept of the 'world within a world.'...Courtyards, creating a world within a world, are translations of these notions in architecture."[11] Goetz was evidently oblivious to this conception of space—just as was Soundara Rajan when he remarked that the same *dhwajastambha* and elephant "are employed to occupy the vacant open court". A Courtyard is by definition a space complete unto itself—not one waiting to be 'occupied' by large foreign objects. This is a concept fundamental not only to an understanding of the Kailas, but of architecture itself.

We may now retrace our steps down the Lankeshvara Cave's stair to the North Aisle. Directly opposite, at its base, is the *vimana's* Nandi Pavilion, on the ground floor of which, facing us, is another dramatic sculpture of Shiva dancing the *tandava*, still retaining much of the painted plaster that once covered it entirely [figure 26]. Dhavalikar attributes this plastering, remnants of which are to be seen on many of the Kailas's sculptures, to a general renovation ordered by the Holkar Queen Ahilyadevi who reigned from 1725 to 1795. This panel too has been severely vandalized. Although a masterful work, it does not display quite the incandescent spark of genius that we have just seen in the Lankeshvara Cave.

Just to its left is a small roofed passageway, about twenty feet square, connecting the temple's North and South Aisles. Its floor is elevated a few steps [figure 27]. Here, facing one another, are two enormous panels, carved in high relief, of the Lord Shiva. To our right (actually on the east face of the Nandi Pavilion's unexcavated 'basement') we see the god in his terror-inspiring aspect as Bhairava, slaying the demon Andhakasura [figures 28 & 29]. Directly opposite, to our left, in an equally large panel, Shiva sits motionless in sublime meditation as Mahayogi, the great yogi [figure 30]. I have called this space the Shiva Passage. Prominently situated at the very centre of the temple, midway between the two stairs leading up to the heart of its *vimana*, these two sculptures together comprise the most powerful and memorable visual presentation of Shiva that the Kailas has to offer.

The *Bhairava* panel combines two related legends. In the first, Shiva has just slain the elephant demon Gajasura, has flayed him, and with four of his ten arms holds the demon's skin above his head in triumph. In the second, he is about to dispatch the still more evil demon Andhakasura (some versions of the myth assert that it was he who had incited Gajasura to do battle with Shiva in the first place). Andhakasura, however, who is visible in the form of a dwarf just to the right of Shiva's head, had been granted a boon that from every drop of his blood that fell to the ground in battle, an equally fierce new demon would arise in his defence. To prevent this, Shiva has enlisted the aid of the 'seven mothers' (*sapta-matrikas*), embodiments of the female dynamic power inherent in the six gods

Brahma, Shiva, Kumara, Vishnu, Varaha, and Indra, together with the terrifying goddess Chamunda, to catch the demon's blood in midair. In addition, he himself holds a bowl for this purpose in his third left hand. The *sapta-matrika*s, their heads long ago broken off, are seen in the lower left corner of figure 28. Shiva's third right hand holds his hourglass-shaped *damaru*, the drum of creation; in his fourth is his fearsome *trisula*, or trident, with which he is about to impale his adversary, and in the last, an elephant tusk.

In this spectacular exploitation of sculptural space, Shiva's flailing arms, the angled posture of his body and of his right leg trampling another demon underfoot, dwarves dancing exuberantly between his legs, his matted hair and the garland of skulls about his neck, and above all the surging thrust of his torso out of the wall [see figure 29], almost fully in the round, vividly portray the power and majesty of the scene. Yet here, as we have seen in the sculptures of Devi Mahishasuramardini and Shiva performing the *tandava*, the deity's face remains serene. In the midst of the battle, Shiva's fourth left arm stretches out to caress the face of his consort Parvati at the lower right. Again, the action is a dream, a *lila,* played out against a background of eternity.

The Mahayogi panel on the east side of the Shiva Passage [see figure 30], though of the same dimensions as the Bhairava (nearly twelve feet high), presents an entirely different, but perhaps equally compelling aspect of the god. His eyes closed and body perfectly still, Shiva sits in deepest meditation on a lotus pad, surrounded by gods, *rishi*s (sages) and musicians. He is the absolute *yogin*, the all-knowing Mahayogi, his majestic form the complete antithesis of Bhairava, facing him across the Passage.

"On his two sides," write Gupte and Mahagan,

> "musicians are shown playing loudly on their instruments. But their noise does not disturb Siva. On the two sides of Siva are shown *sadhus* trying to meditate. They are bound to their seats with *'yoga-pattas'* (bands). But the din and bustle around them disturbs them and makes it impossible for them to concentrate

on anything. This is in great contrast with Siva whom nothing can disturb. But this meditation of Siva causes great consternation among the *asta-dikpalas* (the eight guardians of the quarters). According to the *Siva Purana*, Siva is Creator, Protector and Destroyer. When therefore Siva sits in meditation the world ceases to function; and the guardians of the quarters in great consternation rush to Kailasa, the abode of Siva, to request him to give up his meditation and begin the performance of his triple functions."[12]

Both Bhairava and Mahayogi are splendid works of art in their own right, but it is in their placement here, facing one another across this little space, that their most significant message lies. Shiva is at once both of these aspects. All phenomena, however diverse they may seem, come together in Him, as part and parcel of a single whole. This is the metaphoric message of these great sculptures—and of the space they ennoble.

Notes

1. Kramrisch, Stella. *The Hindu Temple*. 1946. Reprint, Delhi: Motilal Banarsidass, 1976: p. 164.
2. Berkson, Carmel. Ellora, Concept and Style. New Delhi: Abhinav, 1992: p. 93.
3. Burgess, James and James Fergusson. *The Cave Temples of India*. 1880. Reprint, Delhi: Oriental Books, 1965: p. 458
4. *Ibid.*, pp. 451–463.
5. Architectural Survey of India is the national government agency responsible for the management and maintenance of the Kailas and most other major historical sites in India.
6. Zimmer, Heinrich. *Myths and Symbols in Indian Art and Civilization*, ed. Joseph Campbell. 1946. Reprint: Princeton University Press, 1972, p. 155–156.
7. Coomaraswamy, Ananda K. *Introduction to Indian Art*. 1913. Reprint, New Delhi: Munshiram Manoharlal, 1968, p. 73.
8. Zimmer 1972, Op. cit.
9. Dallapiccola, Anna L. *Dictionary of Hindu Lore and Legend*. London: Thames & Hudson, 2002: p. 127. "Name of a destructive aspect of Shiva, in which he devours time and creation, dissolving every kind of life in the ocean of non-existence; from this the new creation emerges and it will eventually return to it."
10. Coomaraswamy, Ananda K. *Introduction to Indian Art*. 1913. Reprint, New Delhi: Munshiram Manoharlal, 1968, p. 71.
11. Pandya, Yatin. *Concepts of Space in Traditional Indian Architecture*. Ahmedabad: Mapin, 2005: p. 14.
12. Gupte, Ramesh and B. D. Mahajan. *Ajanta, Ellora and the Aurangabad Caves*. Bombay: Taraporevala, 1962: pp. 207-8.

Galleries

Stepping back again into the North Aisle, we pass on our right the entrance to the north stair leading to the temple's West Porch. Bending right after a dozen steps it disappears from view. We will climb it in due course, but first let us complete our ground-level *pradakshina*.

31. Ravana cutting off his heads in homage to Lord Shiva, North Gallery

FACING PAGE

32. Marriage of Shiva and Parvati, with Brahma officiating at base, East Gallery

33. East Aisle, looking south from its north end, showing the thirty-foot ceiling overhang

Just around the corner of the stair enclosure, on its north-facing wall, is a carved panel, visible at the left side of figure 51, made up of seven rows of small figures, presenting a continuous linear narrative of episodes from the Mahabharata, one of India's two great epics. (A similar narrative, relating Hinduism's other epic, the Ramayana, occupies a corresponding position on the *vimana*'s south wall.) Diagonally across the North Aisle from the Mahabharata scenes, a short flight of steps leads up to the first of a series of colonnaded galleries, elevated five or six feet above the floor of the Aisles, which encircle the entire east half of the *vimana*. Each of their forty-three bays houses a huge sculpture against its back wall, depicting a scene from the lives of the gods. In the North and East galleries these are primarily drawn from the mythology of Shiva and his consort Parvati; most in the South Gallery are from that of Vishnu. First on our left, as we enter the North Gallery is an image of the *asura* Ravana as a young devotee of Shiva [figure 31]. He has just cut off nine of his ten heads (actually, according to some accounts, these decapitations occurred at 1,000 year intervals), and has placed them in adoration around the god's *lingam*, seen at the top of the panel. Beneath, Ravana kneels with a knife at his throat, ready to cut off his last. But according to legend, Shiva, impressed (or perhaps duped) by his devotion, then appeared to him, restored his heads, and agreed to grant him any boon he desired. Ravana asked first for immortality, but that was beyond even Shiva's power to grant. Thus he asked, considering it beneath his dignity to seek such protection against a mere human, that he might never be killed by any god or demon. Shielded by this immunity, Ravana proceeded to conquer and oppress the worlds of both mankind and the gods. The seed of his destruction had been planted, however. As the Ramayana relates, he was ultimately slain by the great god Vishnu, incarnated in human form for this purpose as the royal prince Rama of Ayodhya.

Most scholars believe the galleries were the last parts of the Kailas complex to be carved, perhaps late in the ninth century, by which time the Kailas's artistic peak had clearly been passed. Goetz considered them reminiscent of "Chola art of the decadence period, and thus probably not earlier than the twelfth or thirteenth century."[1] Some have regarded them as an afterthought, not intended by the

FACING PAGE
34. East Gallery, looking south

ABOVE
35. Elephant sculptures on north side of Vimana's base, looking west from East Gallery

temple's original *sthapati*. It is fair to assert that the sculpture within these galleries is generally of a lower artistic standard than that of the temple's earlier work. Surely some of it is not entirely devoid of merit, however, for instance the panel representing the marriage of Shiva and Parvati [figure 32], in which the four-faced Brahma, seen at the base of the panel, officiates in the ceremony.

Were these galleries part of the original conception of the Kailas's first *sthapati?* Perhaps not. But if they were indeed an afterthought, their result has surely been salutary. The spatial experience of walking through these galleries, though unmentioned by any archaeologist or historian,[2] is among the finest in the temple. Looking south down

36. Base of Vimana, looking southwest from intersection of North and East Galleries

the East (rear) Aisle from the North Gallery [figure 33], a vast stone ceiling soars outward overhead, thirty feet unsupported into space, before the massive cliff face at its outermost edge rises vertically nearly a hundred more to the rim of the Kailas's excavation. A few feet beyond, the stunning East Corridor opens before us, beautifully captured by Peeyush Sekhsaria's camera [figure 34]. The views these galleries present of the central temple, modulating at every bay as we advance from one to the next, offer the finest and most intimate panorama of the Kailas's great frieze of elephants, carved almost completely in the round, fronting the solid plinth. The elephants exemplify not only royal power, but also the tremendous strength required to carry the seemingly ponderous load that rises above them. On the *vimana*'s north, east and south walls, and at its corners, many are shown in fierce combat with lions; at the east wall they stand side by side, facing directly outward [figure 35]. A diagonal view looking southwest from the Galleries' northeast corner [figure 36] shows a bit of the frieze on the *vimana*'s plinth. Unfortunately many of these figures have been severely damaged: a majority of the elephants' trunks are now missing, as well as arms, legs and heads of both elephants and lions. Yet the strength and beauty of what remains intact are extraordinarily powerful.

Whether originally planned or not, from an architectural standpoint these galleries add significantly to the temple's overall conception. Their long vistas of repeating bays provide a powerfully ordered vision of space, a not unwelcome counterpoise to a visual environment that often teems with unbridled movement. Their orientation, parallel to the sides of the temple itself, 'squares off' the ground level plaza from which the *vimana* rises. By no means to be overlooked among the galleries' contributions is the dramatic—intimidating even—impact that is presented to the visitor viewing the *vimana* from the galleries' northeast corner, of 35 million pounds of stone looming just above his head, unsupported, cantilevered thirty feet outward into space!

37. Shikhara, looking north from South Gallery

From the South Gallery the *vimana* appears in yet another manifestation: its *shikhara* now soars above, splashed in sunlight [figure 37]. Below and to the left, our view of it is punctuated by an

38. Vishnu in his man/lion avatar slaying the evil king Hiranyakashyapu, south wall of Vimana, viewed from South Aisle

extraordinary sculpture of Vishnu as Narasimha [figure 38], his body twisted nearly 180 degrees at the waist as he turns to slay the evil king Hiranyakashyapu. Granted a boon protecting him from death at the hand of man or beast, by day or by night, indoors or outdoors, the king was finally slain by Vishnu in his man-lion incarnation (neither man nor beast), at dusk, (neither day nor night), and in the doorway of his castle, (neither indoors nor outdoors). Here the vibrant sculptural style of the Kailas is at its artistic zenith, bursting with angular vigour and life-instilled exuberance.

Notes

1. Goetz, Hermann. "The Kailasa of Ellora and the Chronology of Rashtrakuta Art". In *Artibus Asiae* 15 (1952): p. 106.
2. Berkson, Carmel. *Ellora, Concept and Style*. New Delhi: Abhinav, 1992: p. 87.

Ravana

The South Gallery ends at a narrow door leading to the lowest floor of the Paralanka cave. Passing through it, an archetypal view opens to our right of the Kailas's starkly dramatic sculpture of Ravana shaking Mount Kailasa, described in the opening paragraphs [figure 39]. Here, in perhaps the Kailas's most powerful symbiosis of the built and the unbuilt, the sculpture's fine carving is powerfully juxtaposed with a massive outcrop of virgin stone. Yatin Pandya refers to

39. Ravana shaking Mount Kailasa, south wall of Vimana, looking north from bottom level of Paralanka Cave

juxtapositions such as this as 'Bipolarity of Existence', a conception deeply rooted in traditional Indian architecture, in which "polar opposites reinforce each other: extremes, in which one shapes and gives validity to the existence of the other, and vice versa."[1] Here, the raw rock to the right of the panel coexists with—and gives meaning to—the finely finished carving of the sculpture itself, while the latter contributes meaning to the raw cliff, symbolizing the mountain within which its action is taking place.

A few steps farther along, we come to a short flight of stairs that leads down to the South Court's floor, directly facing the sculpture [figures 40 Ravana (detail) and 41 Shiva with his entourage (detail)]. Once in a while a youngster may be seen nestled in Ravana's lap, as his parents proudly preserve the moment in a snapshot! The entire sculpture is a huge work, nearly twenty feet high, deeply recessed within a plain stone frame reminiscent (as Rowland suggests) of a theatre proscenium.

No work of art in the Kailas better exemplifies the metaphoric wonder that pervades the temple, or better expresses its single, most powerful, defining message. Yet, I believe, it has been widely misunderstood.

The sculpture stands beneath the remains of a stone bridge [figure 42], long ago collapsed, that originally linked the Paralanka cave's middle level to the *vimana*'s south porch. Or so most observers believe. One who does not, however, is K. V. Soundara Rajan, who argues that the Paralanka was carved a quarter century later than the *vimana*, and that the supposed bridge was not a bridge at all, but in fact "a bridge-like extension...that extended almost up to the original cliff face of the courtyard." There it simply dead-ended, facing a mountain of rock. Its *raison d'être,* in Soundara Rajan's view, was to provide a sort of awning over the sculpture "in order to give the appropriate dramatic effect to the cavernous character of the scene." When the Paralanka was carved more than a quarter century later, he says, "the architects had removed this overhanging bridge-like piece projecting from the southern porch, to adjust the facade elevation of this triple storied cave, leaving it more or less in the

40. Ravana (detail of figure 39)

41. Shiva, Parvati and attendants (detail of figure 39)

condition we see it now."[2] Soundara Rajan cites as evidence in support of this scenario the fact that instead of a stone bench (*kakshasana*) at the outer edge of the South Porch, as on the matching porch on the north side of the *vimana*, a detailed examination revealed that no such bench had been incorporated in its design. However, his argument is redundant as this would have been the case whether or not it was conceived as a bridge.

Speaking as one myself, I simply cannot imagine any fellow architect adopting a scheme such as this. How, in the first place, would the outer end of Soundara Rajan's "bridge-like" construction have

been supported, if it stopped short of the cliff beyond? Given the thinness of its remaining stone edge [see figure 42] it could not possibly have been cantilevered twenty feet or so into thin air that he describes, so there must have been a means to support its outer edge. Wooden posts? Stone piers? Cables suspended from the cliff face? Any of these would have resulted in a conspicuously clumsy 'solution.' Soundara Rajan, however, does not address this problem. Second, viewed from above the unsettling human experience of a walkable stone surface leading twenty feet into a blank wall is the last thing a sensible architect would have contemplated under any circumstances, let alone to provide a visual cover that a simple

42. South Porch of Vimana showing the broken bridge, viewed from middle level of Paralanka Cave

wooden or canvas awning would have done just as effectively at a fraction of the cost. Third, if Soundara Rajan had read the account of his 1810 visit to the site by Captain Seely of the Bombay Native Infantry, he would have learned that the ruins of the collapsed bridge were still lying on the ground at that time, strongly suggesting that its fall had been relatively recent. It is hard to imagine, even in India, that the fallen stone would have lain around for more than a millennium after the sculpture was carved!

What Soundara Rajan has done, like Goetz before him regarding the River Goddess complex and North Aisle, is to seize upon a few minor details, combine them with a few dubious assumptions, and produce a conclusion that is clearly off the mark. It is apparent here, as

Dhavalikar has concluded, that the Paralanka must have been carved before or at the same time as the *vimana*, that they were connected by a stone bridge, and that the bridge collapsed some relatively short time before 1810. It is likely as he suggests that the Paralanka served as a storage facility and/or worker housing during the Kailas's creation, as it contains no sculpture, and the bridge would have provided a most useful circulation link throughout this activity. But Dhavalikar, I believe, misses the point of *why* the sculpture was placed under the bridge in the first place. "Its location beneath the rock bridge joining the temple and the first storey of the Paralanka," he says,

> "would suggest that it may not have been carved when the bridge was standing, for the simple reason that the panel under the deep shadow of the bridge would have been constantly in the dark and hence would have lost all of its dramatic effect. In all probability, therefore, it might have been carved after the collapse of the bridge as a result of which the spot became well lighted."[3]

The bridge's shadow, however, was precisely the reason for placing the sculpture beneath it. Depicting an event purportedly having taken place in the deepest recesses of Shiva's own Mount Kailasa, this great panel stands at the very base of the Kailas, the innermost place within this temple that is itself a symbolic model of that very mountain. To grasp fully its metaphoric message, one must recognize that it was never intended to be seen as it appears today, but only from below, where the figures of Shiva and his companions far overhead would have melted away as the viewer's gaze moved upward—perhaps amid the smoky haze of a flaming torch—into the gloom of the bridge's shadow. Even now, as can be seen in figure 39, the upper part of this sculpture appears to dissolve away in the dim light. But to comprehend it fully, as it was originally intended, we must experience it in our imagination as it would have been seen by a worshipper of centuries ago, soaring upward and finally disappearing into mystery, darkness, and sublime symbolism.

These last speculations, I believe, are particularly telling examples of the blind mindset that pervades much of Kailas scholarship.

It is a mindset that seeks out truth from details, rather than from overall conception. It is a mindset that is evident, as I have shown, in misunderstandings of the *sthapati*'s design intent with respect to the temple's entrance, to its River Goddess complex, to its North Aisle, to the Lankeshvara cave, and in other contexts that I will touch upon in the text that follows. It is even to be found in the naming of the temple itself.

Rowland has noted that "as its name implies, [the Kailas] is intended as an architectural replica of the sacred mountain,"[4] a fact that would appear obvious on its face. Dhavalikar and Soundara Rajan, however, do not agree. Dhavalikar states "there is every possibility of the temple having been named 'Kailas'[5] after [the Ravana Shaking Kailas sculpture] as was first suggested by Bhandharkar."[6]

Soundara Rajan ventures farther afield:

> "It is not clear what particularly impelled Krishnaraja to call it 'Kailasa:' Perhaps the lofty stature of the monolith basing the classical poetic imagery tempted him to affix the name of the snowbound Empyrean on the Himalayas. Or, the depiction of the famous theme of Ravana shaking Kailasa, shown almost in the form of a tableaux than of a panel, on the southern wall of the basement storey, made the affixation of this name appropriate in popular mind. Anyway, from a purely canonical angle, it would seem that this name has no *prima facie* connotation, since Kailasa should represent circular shape of sikhara, among the five basic shapes of ancient *silpa* texts, (the square (*Vairaja*) circular (*Kailasa*) elliptical (*manika*), the rectangular (*pushpaka*) and the octagonal (*trivishtapa*). The shape of its *sikhara* was octagonal and not circular. However, probing deeper we see that the shrine was one of the very first at Ellora wherein the *sanctum sanctorum* carried a circular *linga-pitha*, [a *yoni*, or dish representing the vagina, from the centre of which, in Hindu iconography, the lingam typically rises] and if this was the basis, on which the term Kailasa had been applied for it, we see that it was most apposite since once the circular *linga-pitha* came into being, there was practically no looking back and using other variant forms, namely,

> the square and the octagonal and throughout South India, and also perhaps in many parts of the north, the circular *linga-pitha* became ubiquitous. This was perhaps the canonical significance of the term '*Kailasa*'."[7]

Are we truly to believe that the Kailas may have been named for a new shape of stone vagina in its *garbhagriha?*

As suggested early in this study, the Kailas must be seen as a *religious monument* to be fully understood. There are few conceptions more important to this understanding than that the temple in its entirety is a symbolic representation of the home of God. Yet this is an understanding essentially absent from the mindset evidenced by Goetz's misadventures, by many scholars' blindness to the metaphors of the temple's entrance sequence, of the raw cliffs from which the River Goddess complex emerges and those towering over us as we stand awestruck in the North Aisle, their blindness to the symbolism of Ravana's mighty shaking of Mount Kailasa, set deep within the bowels of the mountain's very image—and by Dhavalikar's and Soundara Rajan's misreading of the temple's very name.

Notes

1. Pandya, Yatin. *Concepts of Space in Traditional Indian Architecture*. Ahmedabad: Mapin, 2005: pp. 18–19.
2. Soundara Rajan, K. V. *The Ellora Monoliths*. Delhi: Gian, 1988, p. 158.
3. Dhavalikar, M. K. *Masterpieces of Rashtrakuta Art*. Bombay: Taraporevala, 1983: p. 24.
4. Rowland, Benjamin. *The Art & Architecture of India: Buddhist/Hindu/Jain*. Baltimore: Penguin, 1967: p. 186.
5. Dhavalikar 1983, *Op. cit*.
6. *Ibid.*, p. 50.
7. Soundara Rajan, K. V. *The Ellora Monoliths*. Delhi: Gian, 1988, p. 16–17 (sic).

South Aisle and Court

The Paralanka Cave's three levels are devoid of sculptural embellishment, but compensate for this by the extraordinary range of views they offer of the *vimana*'s south face, and of the South Aisle to both left and right. A new ASI stair climbs to the Paralanka's middle floor, at the same level as the *vimana*'s principal rooms. Some of the finest of these visions of space are to be seen from here, many framed dramatically by the rude stone walls, floors and ceilings of the cave itself. Figure 42, looking north to the vimana's South Porch, shows the broken lip of the fallen bridge, its extreme thinness making it seem a most likely candidate for collapse. Figure 43, looking down and to the left from the Paralanka's topmost level, perhaps conveys some of the spatial excitement to be experienced from here. From left to right are first seen the massive walls of the Paralanka, a bit of its lower floor projecting below; then the South Aisle and Court, with the bases of its *stambha* and Nandi Pavilion. Next is the exterior wall of the south stair to the temple's main level with its *Ramayana* frieze. A corner of the West Porch and the beginning of the band of elephants that encircle the *vimana's* base are also visible. Finally, at the extreme right, the South Porch with the jagged edge of its fallen bridge comes into view.

A final visual treat from the Paralanka is a close-up view of yet another scene from Ravana's chequered career: his abduction of Rama's wife Sita as recounted in the *Ramayana* [figure 44]. It is one of the Kailas's finest and most celebrated sculptures, vibrantly alive with its hugely dramatic diagonal composition, the scene literally bursting out of its frame. Through a ruse engineered by Ravana, Sita has been left unprotected while travelling through the forest in exile with her husband Rama. Ravana has seized her, and is carrying her aloft in his magic chariot toward his castle in Lanka, but the valiant old Jatayu, King of the Vultures, has flown after him in an attempt to rescue her. Ravana turns, sword in hand, and is about to slice off his wings. The crippled bird, fallen to earth, is later discovered by Rama, and tells him what has occurred just before he expires. In this panel Sita stands helpless atop the chariot in the upper right. Her head is broken off, but fortunately the panel has otherwise avoided vandalism, thanks no doubt to its position on the temple wall high above the ground. The panel is visible also just to the left of the temple's South Porch in figure 42.

Another of the Kailas's pitch-black stairs winds its way up to the Paralanka's topmost level, from which delightful variations on all of these scenes may be obtained. A rear room here is crowned by a sort of cupola, rising above the top of the cliffs, that admits a tiny amount of light to its interior. Retracing our steps now down to the South Aisle, we turn left, soon passing the venue of the impromptu *phugdi* game, described above and shown in figure 17. A few more steps bring us to the base of a rebuilt stair, parallel to the cliff face, leading up fifteen feet to the Yajnasala, or Hall of Sacrifice (so called for two small pits

43. South Aisle, looking downward, northwest from top level of Paralanka Cave

in its floor, presumably for sacrificial fires), carved laterally back into the temple's south cliff. Just thirty-seven feet wide and fifteen feet deep, and ignored by many scholars in their descriptions of the Kailas. (Soundara Rajan does not mention it in his 1988 *The Ellora Monoliths,* for instance, nor do Rowland or Brown.) This little cave is nevertheless a unique and totally extraordinary artistic component of the Kailas. Its northern face is open to the South Aisle except for two columns, on each of which stands a life-size *dvarapalika* (female guardian) with a dwarf attendant at her feet [figure 45]. "Standing erect," Carmel Berkson writes, "the guardians are tall, stately and solid...their large heads and faces are as prominent as their figures, complementing the creative power implicit in their extended, bulging hips...A bold bodily curve conveys their energy from head to toe...These symbols of Shakti—the personification of female creative power—are set within the ambience of the Kailasa's world of tumult and riotous action."[1]

Inside, the cave's focus on *shakti* continues. Occupying the cave's left-hand (east) wall is a beautiful group of three female figures [figure 46]—human, since they each have only one set of arms and legs—plus a large *gana* (semi-divine attendant) in the right corner, all carved fully in the round, as is every sculpture within the Yajnasala. The central figure is a personage of obvious importance, probably a queen, seated between two female attendants bearing *chowris* (fly-whisks). R. Sengupta, who studied the Yajnasala in detail, has suggested that she was probably Gamundabbe, queen of the Rashtrakuta King Govinda III, who reigned from 794 to 814 CE. If so, this would obviously suggest that the Yajnasala was carved during this period.[2]

The back (south) wall of the Yajnasala is also devoted exclusively to females, the *sapta matrikas* (Seven Mothers, female aspects of the gods), each with a child in her lap: (from left to right) Varahi, *shakti* of Varaha; Brahmani, *shakti* of Brahma; Maheshvari, *shakti* of Shiva; Kaumari, *shakti* of Skanda; Vaishnavi, *shakti* of Vishnu; an unidentified figure (probably Chamundi, a form of Durga as well as one of the *sapta matrikas*), and finally Indrani, *shakti* of Indra. Unfortunately, most of these figures have been severely vandalized, but the image of

44. Ravana abducting Rama's wife Sita, north wall of Vimana, seen from Paralanka Cave mid-level

FACING PAGE

45. *Dvarapalika* (female guardian), north face of Yajnasala Cave

BELOW

46. East wall of Yajnasala Cave, showing a queen with her attendants

Maheshvari remains a powerful and relatively undamaged sculpture. It is at its right-hand (west) wall, however, that the Yajnasala's most harrowing and unforgettable sculptures are to be seen. The group is dominated by a terrifying, skeletal image of Kala (also known as Yama), god of time and death [figures 47 & 48]. His foot rests on a corpse, with another stretched across his lap. (Yet Kala is regarded by many Hindus as a benign god, who helps his victims to escape from their old, worn out bodies, and enabling them to be born again in fresh new ones.) Seated to his left is his consort Chamundi, depicted as a dishevelled hag, symbolizing death and destruction, and similarly draped with a dead body, as beneath her feet her traditional vehicle, the jackal, gnaws on the thigh of another corpse. A second image of Chamundi peers eerily over Kala's right shoulder. To the right of the seated Chamundi is a life-size figure of a fearsome goddess, probably Durga, mounted on a lion. Here again, despite the presence of the male god, it is the female characters who predominate.

47. Yama, Chamundi and Durga with corpses, west wall of Yajnasala Cave

FACING PAGE
48. Yama, with corpses across his lap

What are we to make of this imagery? Carmel Berkson offers an interpretation:

> "The Hall of Sacrifice (Yajnasala) is nothing short of a living environment, a theatrical setting, a stage for the enactment of the life and death drama of the sacrificial ritual...The unique, high position of the shrine, carved into the southern boundary wall, and its isolation, testifies to the premier role played by these female deities during the Rashtrakuta period. As the *shakta* cults were the single higher religion still demanding human sacrifice, this may well have been the locus of the sacrifice to the goddesses. Only reflected light reaches this subdued and mysterious atmosphere, an echo of dark rites from a distant past... While the *matrikas* receive pride of place on the south wall, the votary is confronted, in front of the west wall with their perpetual associate, the most remarkable figure of Yama and his sprawling victims, with two female lieutenants one of whom is with a lion. The entire shrine was originally hidden behind heavy wooden

49. South face of Vimana, looking north from Yajnasala Cave

doors. Sitting in leisurely fashion yet dignified; provocatively sensuous yet firmly modelled; voluptuous yet independently proud; tall, stately, full with youthful *shakti* power, the queen and her attendants are wrenched out from the geometrical confinement [typical of earlier sculptural styles]. In a bold rupture from the severities of the past [characterized by rigid line-ups of figures in wall-bound friezes], an entirely new idiom reflects vitality and ripeness of feminine attributes which are lusty, forceful, controlling, yet unyielding, expressive of *shakti* power and more than a slight amount of confidence in their own powers of seduction. They are depicted as being full with tremendous life force, precisely because of their massive solidity...But despite all the life force, they were intended to face Yama, the god of death, who grinds up all the living in his domains.

"Separated from the west wall behind them, the Yama group offers no connotations of moral interdictions. It is an ironic and matter-of-fact parable, a pronouncement concerning human capacities of self-deception, ego involvements and the illusory creations of the mind...Death is given pride of place. The hideous, skeletal apparition sits in calm repose of authority, without emotional participation; he is blithely involved in the procedures of devouring all creations, only very recently alive, represented by the horizontal figures spread-eagled across his lap. Beauty of youth, with Apollonian facial features and formalized waves of tresses, [note the "Appollonian" figure draped over Yama's lap in figure 48] is no longer relevant, as even

> the jackals have feeding rights. The lesson for the votary is that not sacrifice, which had been offered in the square floor altars, not the protection of the *matrikas*, nor all the royal power will make the slightest bit of difference for a person wishing to find a way out of the inevitable."[3]

Though contemporary with the three River Goddesses that we have already seen, the artistic conception of these Yajnasala sculptures is totally different. Here the artist has given us a harrowing vision of death in superbly executed, graphic detail, within a composition that is visually fulfilling, yet of the utmost complexity. It is at an opposite pole from the suave, elongated grace of Ganga, Sarasvati and Jamuna, across the way [see figures 9 & 10]. In his *Introduction to Indian Art*, Coomaraswamy writes that while "the modern world, with its glorification of personality, produces works of genius and works of mediocrity following the peculiarities of individual artists, in India the virtue or defect of any work is the virtue of the race in that age."[4] Yet the work of individual Indian artists of every age, as elsewhere throughout the world, has always been marked by differing levels and qualities of genius or mediocrity. That two sculptors, working in the same place, at the same time, and subject to the same rigid theocratic demands of the *shilpashastras*, could produce here two works of genius so different from one another, is an extraordinary reality.

Memorable as is the Yajnasala's incredible sculpture, the magnificent view that this little cave offers across the *vimana* [figure 49] illustrates, perhaps better than from any other viewpoint, both the astonishing richness of the Kailas's carving and the dramatic power of its setting. The view is framed by a rough stone ceiling, thrust out over the scene, and by the temple's ever-present backdrop of raw cliffs. From left to right we see the south *dhwajastambha*, the two story Nandi Pavilion behind it, and the stone bridge spanning the Shiva Passage, linking it to the *vimana*'s West Porch. High above the Porch towers an elegant lion sculpture, carved in place at the very beginning of the excavation process; beneath it, on the face of the South Stair enclosure, is the frieze relating the story of the *Ramayana*, carved perhaps at its very end.

Returning now to the South Aisle, we turn left and descend the few steps to the South Court, passing a major panel of Narasimha slaying Hiranyakashyapu on the south face of the Nandi Pavilion—which, however, does not quite achieve the power of the one we have seen on the *vimana*'s south wall [see figure 38]. A small, nameless cave in the southwest corner of the Court affords a memorable reprise of our first glimpse of the River Goddess complex, directly opposite—its entrance seen through the Gajalakshmi Passage, and the tip of its great arch peeking up above the bridge to the *Gopuram*. The South Court's free-standing elephant is severely mutilated, but still frames an impressive vista of the South Aisle, looking back between its legs, and of the east cliffs in the distance.

Finally at our left, just before we enter the Gajalakshmi Passage to conclude our ground-level *pradakshina*, is a sculptural depiction of *Shiva tripurantaka*, a famous legend in which the God destroys the Three Towns of the *Asuras* with a single arrow. "For it is related," Heinrich Zimmer reports,

> "that Shiva once annihilated and simultaneously redeemed the universe with a single shaft. The demons, titans, or antigods *(asuras)* who are the half-brothers and eternal rivals of the gods, had contrived to gather to themselves the reins of cosmic government. They had been led in this exercise by an austere and crafty tyrant named Maya, who, when he had driven the deities from their seats, constructed three strongholds, one in the firmament, one on earth, and a third in the atmosphere between. All were invincible, and by a feat of magic he amalgamated them into one prodigious center of demon chaos and tyrannical rule. A prophecy made it known that if this incredibly powerful keep were pierced by a single arrow the rule of the antigod would end. But who among the gods could deliver such a blow?"

The Ellora sculpture [figure 50]

> "is a relief of Shiva himself as the archer, in a chariot drawn through the air by divine prancing steeds. The god's left hand elevates the bow; his right, having drawn the string to the lobe of

50. Shiva Tripurantaka, destroying the three fortresses of the *asuras* with a single arrow

his right ear and to the full extent of the shaft, has just released the arrow. His four-headed charioteer is the god Brahma, the creator of the world, and his white bull is seen before them...

"Vigorous and dynamic, the beautiful apparition dashes from the background of the relief with the lightness and irresistible power of a lightning flash in a swift triumphant gesture devoid of static substantiality. Energy is suggested in the backward inclination of the shoulders and in the tension of the outlining curve. The volume of the great chest denotes power. The entire work, indeed, is a display of triumphant strength; for the sculptured figures, in their movement and direction, even unite compositionally with two walls of a corner, which are at an angle of ninety degrees. The relief does not seem to adhere to either surface, but leaps forth from its mother stone, obliterating the distinction between relief and sculpture in the round by the boldness of its plastic style and the almost careless skill of a completely competent craft.

"Hindu sculpture is one of the most magnificent chapters in the whole history both of the world's art and the world's religion—for in Indian civilization there was never a division or fundamental contradiction between art and religion, or between art, religion and philosophic thought. [Its] luxuriant display of religious sculpture is a readily legible pictorial script that conveys, through an elaborate yet readily understood symbolism, not only the legends of popular cult, but simultaneously the profoundest teachings of Indian metaphysics."[5]

Notes

1. Berkson, Carmel. *Ellora, Concept and Style*. New Delhi: Abhinav, 1992: pp. 182–185, (slightly edited)
2. Sengupta, R. "The Yajnasala of Kailasa at Ellora and Identification of Some of its Sculptures." In M. K. Dhavalikar, *Masterpieces of Rashtrakuta Art*. Bombay: Taraporevala, 1983, p. 38.
3. Berkson 1992, *Op. cit.*, pp. 212–216.
4. Coomaraswamy, Ananda K. *Introduction to Indian Art*. 1913. Reprint, New Delhi: Munshiram Manoharlal, 1968: p. xi.
5. Zimmer, Heinrich. *The Art of Indian Asia* (completed and edited by Joseph Campbell). Princeton University Press: 1972: pp. 11–12.

Vimana

Having completed our circumambulation of the entire temple at its base, we may now in good conscience ascend to its main floor: the *vimana*. Two stairs lead to the same place: its West Porch. The only difference we will find in choosing one over the other is the order in which its sculptures are encountered. Arbitrarily, then, let us proceed to the North Stair [figure 51].

Rough-hewn and devoid of any decoration, the stairway rises a dozen steps, then turns to the right and disappears upward. What lies beyond we cannot yet see. For Yatin Pandya it is "a transition from the mundane to the celestial, human to the sacred...The physical act of climbing allegorically emphasizes the ascent to the heavens."[1]

Hermann Goetz, on the other hand, regards the stair as "so clumsily set in that it is quite evidently a later adjustment."[2] Surely it would have been clumsy if this were the grand east portal of a Gothic cathedral in Europe. It is entirely appropriate in eighth century India, however, and in the Kailas itself. Every transitional space within this temple—its Entrance Tunnel, the passages from the North Court to the North Aisle, the stair to the Lankeshvara Cave, the corridor within the Lankeshvara from the top of its stair to its terrace, the 'preview' glimpse within the Lankeshvara of its Shiva Nataraja sculpture, the succession of colonnaded galleries, the stair to the topmost level of the Paralanka Cave, and now the North and South Stairs to the *vimana*—are all deliberately designed as *sequences* of human spatial experience. "Space is conceived and perceived on the basis of movement through it" writes Pandya: "The journey in itself becomes the event."[3]

The human experience of the North Stair is extraordinary indeed. As we continue to climb, a sculptural panel comes into view high overhead: it is Shiva, emerging from his *lingam* to rescue his devotee Markandeya from the clutches of Yama, god of death [figure 52]. According to one version of this legend, Markandeya's father was approached by a god and offered a choice: he could father five worthy sons who would support him comfortably in his old age, or he could have a single son of transcendent holiness—who would however die at the age of just sixteen. He chose the

LEFT

51. Entrance to Vimana's North Stair

RIGHT

52. Shiva rescuing his devotee Markandeya from the clutches of Yama, god of death; west wall of Vimana above North Stair

single son, who grew to become an ardent devotee of Shiva. The sculpture depicts the moment at which Markandeya has just reached this fateful age. At the bottom of the panel, we see him praying to Shiva before his *lingam*, aware of his destiny. Yama stands at the right, holding in his left hand one end of his noose (now broken) that formerly encircled Markandeya's neck. Meanwhile Shiva, responding to his worshipper's prayer, surges from his *lingam*. With his left foot planted firmly on Yama's chest, Shiva holds his *trisula* aloft and is about to impale the god of death on its three prongs. In the story Yama relents, and Markandeya goes on to become for thousands of years a renowned sage, and Shiva's most famous devotee.

53. North Stair; final ascent to Vimana's West Porch

Our stair turns to the right: above us now looms the massive painted ceiling of the temple's West Porch [figure 53], in full view as we look upward from the bend. We ascend. As our head rises above the platform of the floor above (there is no railing here to obstruct our view) an exhilarating vista opens to our right, abruptly dissipating the narrow confinement of the stair. Expanding with each additional step, the view encompasses the entire North Court, the Nandi Pavilion, the *dhwajastambha* and inside face of the temple's front wall, the north cliffs, and the plain beyond. But as we near the platform at the top of the stair, another sculpture on the temple wall to our left demands our attention. It portrays in stone a famous story from the *Ramayana*, related in delightful English prose by Ramesh Menon in his "modern retelling" of the Epic, of the river Ganga's fateful descent to earth [figure 54]:

> "Once, many ages ago, there was a king named Sagara, of the House of Ikshvaku, whose two wives had not been able to bear him a child. Hoping for a son, the three of them sat in penance in the Himalayas for a hundred years. At last a *Maharishi*, or seer possessed of supernatural

powers, appeared 'like a fire on the mountain,' and promised them that for their piety one queen would bear him a single son, who would succeed him on his throne; the other would bear him sixty thousand valiant sons, who however would never become kings themselves. All were soon born, and in due course grew to manhood. In appreciation for his good fortune, Sagara resolved to perform the ultimate act of devotion, an *aswamedha yajna*, or horse sacrifice. In preparation for it he released the selected stallion to run unimpeded wherever he chose, 'daring any king to arrest its careen, and claiming fealty from those whose kingdoms the horse crossed unchallenged.'

"The god Indra, however, did challenge its passage. He seized the animal, and hid it deep in *Patala*, the underworld, in the cave of the *Maharishi* (great sage) Kapila. If the horse was not found and the *yajna* not completed, Sagara's priests informed him, 'calamity will visit the House of Ikshvaku.'

"Summoning his sixty thousand sons, Sagara ordered them to seek out and return the horse, wherever it might be. They searched far and wide, across land and sea, but could find no trace of the animal. Finally, they ventured down the spiralling paths of the twilight realms. They came to a dark cavern, and, from within it, heard the whinny of a horse in tether. In they plunged, and saw Kapila, seated in the posture of the lotus, his eyes shut, absorbed in meditation. Beyond him was their father's white horse, tied to a tree.

"'Thief!' they roared, and rushed at Kapila with their weapons raised. The sage's eyes flew open to see who dared disturb his trance, and instantly those sixty thousand sons of Sagara were made ashes; for they all plunged into that unequal encounter in brash, foolhardy waves. When all of them were ashed, Kapila shut his eyes again with a sigh, as if nothing of moment had happened. He went back into his meditation.

"After many years, Sagara sent his grandson, Anshuman, to Kapila's cave to seek the release of his lost sons' souls through *tapasya*, an offering of water for the dead. As he had gone to Kapila in peace and respect, the sage offered no objection—but there was no water to be found anywhere in *Patala*.

54. River Ganga's fateful descent to Earth, west wall of Vimana facing West Porch

"As he ranged those dark labyrinths in quest of water, Anshuman heard a sound of vast wings. Garuda flew down to him. Garuda said to the distraught youth, 'No common water will wash away the sins of your uncles. They violated the earth goddess and outraged the spirits who are her guardians. Only the waters of Himalaya's daughter who flows through the stars can purify their souls. You must bring the Ganga down to wash their ashes; only then will they find deliverance. But it is not yet time for the sacred river to flow on earth. Take your horse home to your grandfather. He waits anxiously for you, and the *aswamedha* must be completed.'

"Anshuman did as Garuda had asked. Sagara completed the *aswamedha*, but he was a broken man, and left his kingdom to his one remaining son, who ruled well in his place. Eventually Anshuman ascended to the throne. He also was a just ruler, as was his son Dilipa, but none of the three were able to find time to perform the penances that might have released those sixty thousand souls. Meanwhile the curse on the Ikshvakus continued to grow stronger every day: now Dilipa's heir Bhagiratha was unable to father a son of his own, and it appeared that the great royal line would soon come to an end.

"Bhagiratha finally recognized that the curse must be exorcized at its root. Giving up his kingly duties, he retreated to the mountains, and sat in excruciating penance for a thousand years. At last Brahma appeared to him, promising to grant any request.

"Bhagiratha, barely able to speak, finally said 'Father of worlds, grant that I may be able to perform *tapasya* for my ancestors with the waters of the Ganga, and that they attain Heaven. Brahma, grant also that I have a son to continue the line of Ikshvaku.' Brahma replied 'You will have a noble son, but if Ganga comes down into the world, who will break her fall? The very earth will be shattered. You must petition Shiva to break her fall!'

"After Bhagiratha had fasted in Shiva's name, living on just air for a year, the Great God of Gods appeared before the Ikshvaku king. Shiva said 'You should not have to sit in penance for a cause as just as yours. I am pleased with your devotion to your ancestors. I will break Ganga's fall, and her pride as well.'

"When Brahma told Ganga that she must flow to earth, she protested: 'The earth will perish from this madness, for there is no one who can bear my descent!' But she could not disobey Brahma. On the appointed night, with all the gods in attendance to watch the scene, suddenly a deafening roar shook the firmament. Bhagiratha saw her coming: she was a sheet of silver, filling the night sky. He shut his eyes with a prayer. Like a cosmic flood she came hurtling down the Milky Way, laughing as she did: she was amused that Brahma had not cared to heed her warning. But then another figure loomed beside Bhagiratha: Shiva, the Lord of the Night. Ganga swept on, and only Shiva knew what was in her arrogant heart. Exhilarated by her plunge down the constellations, she thought to herself 'I will show Shiva who I am. I will thrust him down into *Patala*!'

"With a crash like thunder in the galaxy, Ganga fell straight down on Siva's hallowed head. Bhagiratha shut his eyes, certain that this was the end. Even the *Devas* above fell silent; they, too, did not believe anyone could survive that crystal cataract. A hush fell on earth and sky. But not a drop, let alone a deluge, fell on the terrified Bhagiratha. Shiva still stood smiling, lustrous in the moonlight. But she, endless river, had vanished: she was lost in Shiva's matted hair. And struggle as she would, she could find no way out from where she was absorbed like a water drop. One drop in the ocean that was He.

"At last, drop by drop, Shiva wrung Ganga down onto the earth. High on the Himalayan tableland a pool formed, gleaming in the rising sun, made of the droplets of the chastened river of heaven. The pool grew into a lake and the lake flowed into seven streams. The seventh followed Bhagiratha's chariot, which he rode like the wind to the place where his sixty thousand haughty ancestors had long ago entered the underworld.

"The earth yawned open. As Bhagiratha watched, hardly daring to breathe, Ganga swirled down into the abyss, and Sagara's ancestors rose from their ashes in sudden spirit fire, their astral bodies purified, their long ordeal ended. Blessing him in sixty thousand ringing voices, they rose into heaven. The curse on their Ikshvaku line had ended."

In this sculpture [see figure 54] Shiva is portrayed with four arms: the front right holds out a lock of his hair to receive Ganga's waters, while the rear one rests casually on his hip; his front left arm stretches out to rest gently on the shoulder of his consort Parvati while the rear one holds aloft his *damaru* (an hourglass-shaped drum). Ganga is seen in human form at the top of the frame, flanked by flying divinities; below, her body morphs into a torrent. Bhagiratha stands in the upper left corner, hands clasped above his head in prayer. At the left edge a sage, perhaps Kapila, is seen drinking of the stream as it passes downward to the ashes of Sagara's sons, releasing their souls from the bondage of Kapila's curse.[4]

To the right of this panel is the sole entrance to the Kailas's *mandapa,* or great hall. Before venturing into it, however, we may choose to turn right, descend a few steps, and cross the bridge over the Shiva Passage to the Nandi Pavilion. Within it, Shiva's mount, the bull, stands on the temple's principal axis, looking along it through the *mandapa* to the symbol of his Lord in the *garbhagriha*, the Kailas's innermost inner sanctum beyond. The bull figure that now occupies this space [figure 55] was not carved in place and is undoubtedly not original, nor is it of any particular artistic distinction. Intimate glimpses of both *dhwajastambhas* and their exquisite, delicately carved faces are to be seen through the Pavilion's two side windows. Straight ahead, a second bridge crosses the Gajalakshmi Passage to the upper floor of the *gopuram.* Here we may walk right or left onto the open top of the Kailas's massive front wall, from which celebrated views back through the great North and South Aisles to the massive east cliffs in the distance may be obtained. Yet I would offer the caveat that these long-range views of the cliffs do not approach the power that one can experience standing directly beneath them.

Retracing our steps to the West Porch, two more sculptures, to the right of the *mandapa* door, are deserving of notice. The first, called *Lingodbhava* [figure 56] shows Shiva emerging from a column (*lingam*) of fire. At the lower left Vishnu, in his incarnation as a boar, dives down seeking its base, while Brahma, at the top right corner, flies upward seeking its top. Neither can be found, however, and Vishnu and Brahma are thus forced to acknowledge the supremacy of Shiva. To the right of this panel is a framed figure of Brahma, seated on a lotus [figure 57]. Dhavalikar describes it as "somewhat crude," and suggests that it may have been installed by Queen

55. Interior of Nandi Pavilion, showing the Nandi image and part of the north Dhwajastambha's south face

FACING PAGE
56. Lingodbhava, west wall of Vimana facing West Porch

57. Lord Brahma, west wall of Vimana facing West Porch

FACING PAGE
58. Mandapa interior, showing columns

Ahilyadevi as part of her eighteenth century renovation project.[5] True or not, however, I find this three-faced image to possess a certain pristine power.

The tall door to the *mandapa* is centred on the temple's longitudinal (east/west) axis, and flanked by huge figures of Ganga and Jamuna, both unfortunately now headless. Removing our shoes and jamming them in among the dozens of pairs lining the steps to it, we enter to find ourselves in a hall nearly identical in plan and layout to that of the Lankeshvara's principal space. Both are approximately fifty feet square, their ceilings supported by a cluster of four elegantly carved square columns in each corner [figure 58]. Both are divided into quadrants by wide transverse and longitudinal aisles, intersecting at the room's centre, their crossings emblazoned by sculptures overhead. And yet spatially the two rooms could not be more different. Compare figure 22, the interior of the Lankeshvara, with figure 58, the *vimana*'s *mandapa*: the former, as we have seen, is a focused, *horizontal* space, pointing the way; the latter, nearly twice its height, a dramatically designed *vertical* space of arrival.

Straight ahead through a second doorway, again flanked by headless River Goddesses, stands the Kailas's ultimate symbol: Shiva's lingam, illuminated by an ever-burning oil lamp [see figure 60]. Or at least it used to be. The light is electric now, and no doubt turned off after the day's stream of visitors has departed and the temple's door has been locked for the night. But there is nothing to prevent us from seeing the flickering light of an ancient torch in our imagination, dancing in reflection from the lingam's smooth surface, "bedaubed with red ochre and sweet scented oil, and strewed with odoriferous flowers," as Captain Seely found it in 1810.[6]

Before we enter this sacred *garbhagriha*, however, let us take a closer look at the *mandapa* itself, and its satellite spaces. The great hall is dimly lit, receiving only feeble rays of light from its doors and the perforated stone grilles of its six little windows: our eyes need time to adjust. As they do, a beautiful sculpture of Shiva dancing on a dwarf, attended by Parvati and musicians, comes into view on the ceiling above the crossing of the two central aisles [figure 59]. The transverse aisle ends left and right at doors to the temple's North and South Porches. The North Porch, enclosed by stone benches, often offers a peaceful retreat from the bustle of the *mandapa*, as well as views of the entire North Aisle (and now, alas, of the bat fence across the front of the Lankeshvara's terrace.) Left and right of the door on the exterior are fine sculptural representations of the Andhakasura and Mahishasuramardini legends. The door to the South Porch provides access to the remains of the broken bridge, and is flanked right and left by scenes from the Ramayana: the fight between the monkey brothers Vali and Sugriva, and a close-up view of the magnificent sculpture of Ravana abducting Rama's wife Sita [see figure 44].

In the extreme northeast and southeast corners of the *mandapa*, doorways open to the Kailas's final and most holy *pradakshinapatha*, or path of circumambulation. The verticality of the *mandapa*'s interior has set the tone for this outdoor space: as we step into it, Pandya writes, "the space is directed heavenward in the upward sweep of the *shikhara*."[7] Five subsidiary shrines, each a copy in miniature of the principal *shikhara*, are ranged along the outer edge of the U-shaped pathway. For the devout, treading it is an obligatory rite to be performed before entering the *garbhagriha*. There is another compelling reason to venture here, however. Towered over on three sides by the Kailas's tallest cliffs, the *pradakshinapatha* offers

59. Mandapa interior, showing sculpture on ceiling at central crossing of aisles

60. Mandapa interior:
entrance to Garbhagriha

a unique touch of spatial drama. One by one as the visitor proceeds along this route the five shrines and the *shikhara* itself modulate in seemingly infinite variety, splayed against a constantly changing backdrop of looming cliffs, here closer to the *vimana* than at any other point in its periphery [figures 61 & 63]. We have seen these cliffs from below, but only here do we confront them at mid-height. As in the *lingodbhava* sculpture we saw as we entered the *mandapa* from the West Porch, their summit is out of sight far above, and their base hidden from our view far below.

Before leaving this space, I cannot fail to mention the view shown in figure 62, looking back across the North Aisle toward the *vimana's* North

FACING PAGE

61. *Pradakshinapatha* encircling the Shikhara, looking southeast

RIGHT

62. Vimana's North Porch and Lankeshvara Terrace (2009), looking northwest from *Pradakshinapatha*

Porch and the Lankeshvara's terrace. This view, I believe, epitomizes a crucial essence of the Kailas's design: the deliberate visual overlay of the temple's carved stone against a background of its ubiquitous raw cliffs. As a design device, it is similar in conception to the scene shown in figure 39, in which fine carving and raw stone at the base of the Ravana sculpture are deliberately juxtaposed. Here, however, the juxtaposed elements are huge architectural members, splayed visually against vast cliffs. The visual concept is the same; the scale is entirely different. To quote Pandya once again, it is "existence by negation, exemplified in traditional Indian architecture through symbiosis of the built with the unbuilt." Indian architecture," he adds, "often is the architecture of the unbuilt. The unbuilt [raw or unsculpted surfaces] is defined by the built [sculpted or finished surfaces], while the built subsists through the unbuilt...Coexistence of the raw with the finished faces of the rock give meaning to the carved components."[8]

Figure 62 displays just one among dozens of these juxtapositions with which the Kailas abounds. They are no accident. They are deliberate, essential elements of its design, deeply rooted in Indian architectural tradition. They are to be found everywhere throughout the temple. They appear prominently in this study in its frontispiece, and in figures 1, 2, 3, 5, 8, 12, 13, 19, 20, 21, 26, 33, 36, 37, 38, 39, 42, 43, 44, 45, 46, 52, 61, 62 & 63. Yet one searches in vain for a single reference to these elements among the great majority of scholarly descriptions of the Kailas. Truly, this temple is a *misunderstood masterwork*.

Completing our circuit of the *pradakshinapatha* and re-entering the Kailas's great hall, we come again before the *garbhagriha*, and the visual symbol it harbours within its austere cubical volume: Shiva's *lingam* [see figure 60]. Obviously this vertical, cylindrical shaft is a phallus, and it rises here, as is customary wherever Shiva is worshipped, from the centre of a yoni, a dish-shaped stone vessel symbolically representing the vagina. Thus it is doubly sexual: *lingam* and *yoni* together represent the combined male and female forces of creation itself.

63. *Pradakshinapatha,* view looking southeast

Speaking of the *lingam*, Seely had this to offer (or perhaps to decline to offer):

> The worship of this stone, with the ceremonies observed, need not be detailed: they are of an impure kind. It is an emblem of the generative power...The following observation of an oriental writer, whose name has escaped my memory, sufficiently elucidates the subject to preclude the necessity of my going further into the disgusting detail: "It seems never to have entered the heads of the Indian legislator and people, that anything so natural could be grossly obscene."

What moral message (if any) this forgotten writer may have intended here I am not sure, but what is clear from it is that to the Hindu, or at least to the Hindu of the eighth century, the activities of creation, human and godly, were entirely natural—and in no way "obscene." The conception that human sexual activity might be inherently obscene was exclusively the product of a foreign culture. For Hindus, it "never entered their heads."

Within the psyche of virtually every Westerner, I believe, there is embedded some link that inextricably intertwines his or her innermost conceptions of sex, shame and guilt. If we are to comprehend these symbols of Shiva, the *lingam* and the *yoni*, as does a Hindu worshipper, we need to set these aside. "Instead of seeking to constrain these strange conceptions into the delimiting frames with which we are familiar," says Heinrich Zimmer, "we must let their profound strangeness guide us to an understanding of the unconscious limitations we place on ourselves, through our own conceptions of the mysteries of existence."[9] "When the Hindus worship the *linga*," Alain Daniélou explains, "they do not deify a physical feature, they merely recognize the divine, eternal form manifest in the microcosm...Just as we worship the Sun, the giver of light, the sum of all individual eyes, so also in the *linga* we worship Shiva, who pervades all generative

64. Worshippers at the Lingam in the Garbhagriha

powers. It is not a particular eye we worship and of which we make images but the Sun, the eye totality, the giver of sight, the source of visibility. Similarly it is the Shiva totality which is worshipped and of which images are made."[10] The generative powers that Shiva embodies and Hindus worship are openly expressed as well in sculpture and painting. *Mithuna* couples in innumerable postures of sexual intimacy are found everywhere, especially in temples, including the Kailas, (although they are not as prominent here within the artistic repertoire as at many other sites), and are often interpreted as metaphors for the relationship between mankind and the divine. The female body is generally depicted in art naked above the waist, with unabashedly broad hips and "breast orbs proffered from the chest...symbols of her being, vessels of her plenitude, emblems which she carries."[11]

The *garbhagriha*, a little room nearly cubical in volume and completely unadorned save for its symbol of the Absolute, the *lingam* at its very centre, is the culmination of a devout Hindu's spiritual journey through this temple to an ultimate comprehension of God and Man. Whatever our own background or beliefs may be, perhaps we could share some small measure of his experience. Even Captain Seely, down-to-earth British soldier that he was, proved not immune to the power of this place. On page 150 in his account of his 1810 visit to Ellora, published in 1824, he reported that

> It was my intention to have slept in the great hall of the Keylas, and my couch was placed there, with one of my Siphauees[12] as sentry in the portico, but sleep never came...the gloomy solemn silence that reigned all around after nightfall became oppressively heavy. It was not the pleasing positive melancholy that steals over the mind when viewing these wonders by daylight; it was not fear nor dread, but the imagination brought on by the solitariness and grandeur of the place, and of the mighty race who formed it, which led the mind back to an unknown age, with all its train of reflection on the mutability of human affairs...Surely the *Brahman* could not have designed a fitter place for meditation, or to fix the mind of his worldly or wandering disciple. Nothing can be better adapted to estrange the soul from all mundane ideas than the deep gloom of these temples at the hour of midnight.

I thought about "beating a retreat" to my tent. What must be the feelings of the ignorant superstitious native, who attributes all these temples to divine origin? The Hindoo votary must have been skeptical and lethargic enough who was not impressed with religious awe and superstitious fear, while offering up his orisons at these sacred shrines, acted upon by the delusions of midnight music, innumerable lights of scented oils, the prayers and singing of the priests, and the fierce-looking deities staring him in the face from every direction, in either a mystical, allegorical, or legendary character; and to crown the scene of worship, the glorious canopy of Heaven, with its unknown worlds and millions of lights...Although the Hindoos' ideas and observances are totally different from ours, the same is the tendency of his prayers and offerings to "The Great First Cause, least understood."[13]

Previously (page 113) Seely had concluded that Hinduism's adherents were

the most superstitious people on earth, with the most impossible and absurd mythology...it is an interminable subject, and one that after the deepest research and closest investigation, produces neither amusement nor information, being monstrous lies and fabled imposture from beginning to end.[14]

In the concluding sentences of his description of that night in the great hall, Seely teeters for an instant on the cusp of an "Aha!" moment of acknowledging a belief system utterly foreign to his own Christian upbringing. That he was never quite able to achieve that "Aha!"—and perhaps even felt a twinge of disappointment in his inability to do so—is reflected in a still later passage in his account (page 276), in which he quotes "Mr. Maurice, the author of a valuable treatise on Indian antiquities:"

Concerning the extravagant mythological details of the Hindoos, I must remark that, however wild and romantic the language of which they are clothed, this fact may be depended upon, that there in general lies concealed at the bottom some physical meaning, or deep philosophical truths.' I only know that with much industry, a

> knowledge of the language, and the best local information, I never had the good fortune to arrive at such a conclusion.[15]

The same quandary besets many non-Hindus today, exposed for the first time to—and trying to comprehend—a vast conglomeration of values and conceptions fundamentally different from their own.

None of these values, this comprehension, these conceptions are capable of being conveyed directly through words, or sounds, or through painting or sculpture. They can only be transported from one human mind to another through example: parable: metaphor. Everything in and about the Kailas—the mountain from which it is hewn, the vast excavation from which its *vimana* rises and the great cliffs that enclose it, its architectural forms, its vibrant sculptures and the legends they portray, its symbols, and the astonishing quality of its space—is metaphor. The Kailas, like every Hindu temple, is itself a metaphor—not only for God's presence, but for the entire world of God and Mankind: *the world in a likeness.*

Notes

1. Pandya, Yatin. *Concepts of Space in Traditional Indian Architecture*. Ahmedabad: Mapin, 2005: p. 62.
2. Goetz, Hermann. "The Kailasa of Ellora and the Chronology of Rashtrakuta Art". In *Artibus Asiae* Vol. 15 No. 1 & 2 (1952): p. 96
3. Pandya 2005, *op. cit.*, p. 20.
4. Menon, Ramesh. *The Ramayana*. New York: North Point Press, 2001: pp. 35–41. This account of the 'Descent of the Ganga' is borrowed, largely intact, from Ramesh Menon's luxuriant modern retelling of the Ramayana.
5. Dhavalikar, M. K. *Masterpieces of Rashtrakuta Art*. Bombay: Taraporevala, 1983: p. 30.
6. Seely, Captain John B. *The Wonders of Ellora*. London: G. & A. Whitaker, 1824: p. 150.
7. Pandya 2005, *op. cit.*, p. 70.
8. *Ibid.*, p. 19.
9. Zimmer, Heinrich. *Myths and Symbols in Indian Art and Civilization*, ed. Joseph Campbell. Princeton University Press, 1972: p. 12.
10. Daniélou, Alain. *Hindu Polytheism*. New York: Bollingen Foundation, 1964: p. 227. The last three sentences of this quotation are taken by him from Karapatri, Lingopasana-rahasya.
11. Kramrisch, Stella. *The Hindu Temple*. 1946. Reprint, Delhi: Motilal Banarsidass, 1976, p. 15.
12. An Indian soldier under British command, now usually spelled *sepoy*.
13. Seely 1824, *op. cit.*, p. 150.
14. *Ibid.*, p. 113.
15. *Ibid.*, p. 276.

The World in a Likeness

In 1947, Ananda K. Coomaraswamy published a brief article entitled *An Indian Temple: The Kandarya Mahadeo.*[1] The body of the article, however, contains no mention of this famous eleventh century temple, located at Khajuraho in Madhya Pradesh. In his introductory paragraph, Coomaraswamy explains that his "true subject is *the* Hindu temple, irrespective of period and relative complexity or simplicity." The Hindu temple, he tells us, is "a microcosm, the world in a likeness." The Kandarya Mahadeo is thus a metaphor not only for every Hindu temple, but for the entire world as well.

The world of man, in Hindu thought, is conceived as round, as it would appear to a person from atop a tall tree in the middle of a vast open plain, his view stretching away unboundedly in every direction to a 360 degree horizon. The world of the gods, however, is an ordered one, conceived geometrically in two dimensions as a square, or in three dimensions as a cube. Their world is oriented in conformance with movements of the celestial bodies: most prominently, its cardinal directions are established by the sun's daily travel from east to west, and its annual traverse to and from its summer and winter solstices in the north and south.[2]

This sacred, ordered world is symbolized by a square diagram, a *vastupurusamandala*[3] [illustration C], within which is inscribed the figure of *Purusa*, the primal "Existence,"[4] or "The Being of Immortal Substance", seated in meditation, whose body, according to the *Rigveda*,[5] was dismembered and sacrificed by fire to create the terrestrial world and all life within it. We are all the descendants of *Purusa*.

> *From that sacrifice in which everything was offered, the melted fat was collected, and made into those beasts who live in the air, in the forest, and in villages.*
>
> *From that sacrifice in which everything was offered, the verses and chants were born, the metres were born from it, and from it the formulas were born.*

Horses were born from it, and those other animals that have two rows of teeth, cows were born from it, and from it sheep and goats were born.

When they divided [Purusa,] into how many parts did they apportion him? What do they call his mouth, his two arms and thighs and feet?

His mouth became the Brahmin; his arms were made into the Warrior, his thighs the People, and from his feet the Servants were born.

The moon was born from his mind; from his eye the sun was born. Indra and Agni came from his mouth, and from his vital breath the Wind was born.

From his navel the middle realm of space arose; from his head the sky evolved. From his two feet came the earth, and the quarters of the sky from his ear. Thus they set the world in order.[6]

"Cosmic speculation and the body of man", Michael Meister tells us, "were made into a formal homology" in the *Atharvaveda*, dating from early in the first millennium BCE. "[But] it is in fact only in the time of Varahamihira's *Brihat-Samhira*, written in the sixth century CE, that the use of something like a *vastupurusamandala* to plan cities and buildings was first designated. [Varahamihira begins his treatise by saying] "to gratify clever astrologers, I now proceed to compose a work on the art of building, such as it has been transmitted from the Creator to our days, through an unbroken series of sages." After describing *Purusa*'s original sacrifice, he instructs architects to divide the *vastupurusamandala* into eighty-one squares by drawing ten lines from east to west and ten others from north to south. In his next thirteen verses he discusses the placement of 45 deities into these squares, over the body of the *vastupurusa*. (These lines have been omitted from illustration C for clarity.) According to Kramrisch the drawing of such a *mandala* soon became (and still is) an indispensable prerequisite to the building of a temple, and that mastering its meanings and execution is the first responsibility of the Hindu architect.[7]

Beyond its architectural utility, however, the *vastupurusamandala* conveys another metaphoric message. All of Varahamihira's 81

illustration C. The Vastupurusamandala

squares, and all of his 45 deities, were subsumed beneath *Purusa*'s meditating form: they are one within Him. His body, shown in illustration C, is that of a human being: we too, all of us, are one within Him. His meditation, in Hindu thought the ultimate, insuperable force,[8] shows us the path to final release: the path to the Absolute. Turning again to Coomaraswamy's words, "not only are temples made with hands the universe in a likeness: man himself is likewise a microcosm and a 'holy temple' of the City of God." Man himself is one with the Absolute.

Varahamihira was not merely summing up a millennium of building, but marking a major transition. A new practice of stone construction to make temples to shelter images of deities was just beginning, and the utility of the *vastupurusamandala* was about to be given new life.[9]

The Kailas, begun just two centuries after the *Brihat-Samhita*, was certainly an important architectural example of this new wave—perhaps *the* most important. But neither the Kailas nor the newly recognized potential of the individual human being, symbolized by the *vastupurusamandala*, emerged suddenly from the blue. They were integral manifestations of the new spirit of their time, in which ordinary people finally became fully enfranchised Hindu worshippers, and sculptors thrust aside the strictures of the past to produce a flood of vibrant new art. Hinduism's popularity exploded throughout all levels of Indian society, leaving Buddhism—and much of Hinduism's own Vedic heritage—in its wake. The *bhakti* devotional movement, *darshan* and the newly available *Puranas*[10] all reflected—or inspired—a surge of popular enthusiasm in which everyone could participate.

Perhaps, in retrospect, the greatest contribution of this age has been its magnificent legacy in stone: a vast outpouring of artistic expression never equalled, before or since, in the Indian subcontinent. As Micaela Soar puts it,

> One of the supreme achievements of artistic creativity on earth, one sees at Ellora the external manifestation of a religious tradition of extraordinary power—a tradition which was able

> both to embrace the sophisticated philosophy of the high caste Brahmin and at the same time to retain the vital elements of the earlier simpler and popular worship of mother/river/earth goddesses, and to attract devotees through the whole spectrum of Hindu worship, from ascetics to kings, from the humble peasant to the highest caste of Brahmin.[11]

"The mountain is the totality," writes Carmel Berkson: "all forms are born from it. The caves are from the mountain."[12] From the outside, the most striking feature of the Kailas, and indeed of every temple dedicated to Shiva, is its *shikhara*: its mountain [see figure 5].

> "Beneath the apex of its dome, the house of God rests on this earth whose extent, architecturally, is covered by the *vastupurusamandala*. In it, the temple has its plan, prognosis and projection on the [ground's] surface. [From its topmost finial] downward the temple spreads the rich folds of its cloak, the sheath of its pillar, its superstructure and walls. It extends in all directions, has no façade but is oriented. From its hem or perimeter upwards and inwards it connects all the directions of space and all the constellations in time, in a sumptuous fabric.[13]

Centred deep beneath this tower's peak is a cave, the temple's *garbhagriha*, its sanctum of ultimate mystery. Perfectly square in plan and cubical in volume, totally devoid of embellishment save only for the lingam that rises in its very centre [see figures 60 & 64], it is the perfectly ordered form of the realm of God.

From the earliest beginnings of Hindu thought, the mountain and the cave have symbolized God's presence. The mountain, solid and open, and the cave, empty and hidden, are metaphoric opposites that together reveal the Absolute.

The Kailas is an entire environment, that envelops the visitor, inviting him to leave behind the illusory world of material things, and leading him, step by step, on a spiritual journey that culminates in the understanding that all phenomena are aspects of a single whole: a single reality; a single Absolute. Entering the *garbhagriha* we take the final step in this journey. It is the temple's sanctum of ultimate mystery: the cavity of the heart: our own heart. It is the dark womb[14] of the mountain that we re-enter to find the light[15]—symbolized by the ever-burning lamp within—and from which we emerge spiritually reborn.[16] It is the centre where we are made whole,[17] where we discover the inseparable unity of the material and the spiritual,[18] and where the universe assumes a single form[18] symbolized by the lingam. It is the place where we realize that we ourselves are one with God [figure 65].

But it is not only the lingam here that symbolizes the Absolute: the inner space—the *akasha*, the "all-pervasive, subtlest element of space"[19] itself, that this pristine cubical chamber encloses, is the ultimate metaphor for the Reality, the Wisdom, the Infinity that is Brahman: the Absolute.[21] Within the *garbhagriha* we discover that the inner space of our own heart, our innermost being—our *atman*—is one with the vast outer space of the terrestrial world, just as this tiny cave's bare interior is one with the "sumptuous fabric" of the tower that sheathes it.

> As far, indeed, as the vast space outside extends the space within the heart. Within it, indeed, are contained both heaven and earth, fire and wind, sun and moon, lightning and the stars, both what one possesses here and what one does not possess – all is contained therein.[22]

If the cave is indeed *of the mountain*, as Berkson says, then the *garbhagriha* of the Kailas is an unparalleled metaphor for the presence of the Absolute. For the Kailas, unlike any other Hindu shrine, is itself a cave of the mountain: carved from it in its entirety. Its *shikhara* as well is a mountain—Shiva's mountain—carved within the cave that is carved from the mountain. And the *garbhagriha*, buried beneath the *shikhara*, is a cave carved from a mountain carved from a cave carved from a mountain. As Baumer observes, all of this is uniquely symbolic of the spiritual process from which it was born: a "spiritual process which does not consist in creating something new (an outer structure), but in opening or uncovering the inner space which is already there."[23] And of which we—every one of us—is a living part.

FOLLOWING PAGES
65. Worshippers at the Lingam in the Garbhagriha

Notes

1. Coomaraswamy, Ananda K. "An Indian Temple: The Kandarya Mahadeo". In *Art in America* 35 (1947), pp. 285–292. Reprinted in *Architectural Theory*, ed. Michael Meister (1995).
2. Kramrisch, Stella. *The Hindu Temple*. 1946. Reprint, Delhi: Motilal Banarsidass, 1976: p. 17n.
   Kramrisch points out that the square does not refer to the shape of the Earth, but rather connects the four points established by these primary pairs of opposites. Astronomy and astrology are highly developed and intimately related sciences within Hinduism, and, of course, involve the observed movements of a host of celestial bodies, not only those of the Sun.
3. *Vastu* means "bodily existence," or by extension architecture (Kramrisch); *mandala* means sacred diagram.
4. Kramrisch 1946, *Op. cit.* Kramrisch's term.
5. The *Rigveda* is the first and most important of the four *Vedas* (the others are the *Samaveda, Yajurveda,* and *Atharvaveda*). Collections of ancient hymns, they are the oldest and most sacred written texts of Hinduism, and together comprise the most ancient scriptures of any religion active today. Their dates of composition are not known, but are generally believed to have been at least a millennium before Christ, perhaps as many as four millennia.
6. *Rigveda*, 10.90 (8-14) from O'Flaherty, Wendy Doniger. *The Rig Veda*. London: Penguin, 1961. According to O'Flaherty this myth is of Indo-European origin: "The dismemberment of the Norse giant Ymir is the most striking parallel," she says, "but there are many others." The hymn is also the foundation of Hindu society's division into its four principal castes: *Brahmins*, (priests), *Kshatriyas* (warriors), *Vaishyas* (traders and farmers) and *Shudras* (servants).
7. Kramrisch 1946, *Op. cit.*, p. 39. Kramrisch continues: "These movements, rites and meanings are not accessory or mere accompaniment to the building itself. They go into the making of a Hindu temple, its shape and proportion and that of every carved detail and every figure, each in its proper place, with the rhythms and gestures appropriate to it." Obviously this was written with a structural temple in mind, and her references to "stretching the cord" or laying out the temple's plan on the ground before commencing construction, and to its foundation bearing weight may not apply to the Kailas. Nevertheless, the principles underlying her statement are fully pertinent to it.
8. Coomaraswamy, Ananda K. *Essays in Architectural Theory*, ed. Michael Meister. Oxford University Press, 1969, p. 103..
9. Meister, Michael W. "Vastupurusamandalas: Planning in the Image of Man". In *Mandalas and Yantras in the Hindu Tradition*, ed. Gudrun Bühnemann. Brill, Boston and Leiden, 2002, p. 254.
10. The eighteen principal *Puranas*, or "Stories of Old," written in Sanskrit in the first millennium of the Christian era, are to a large extent assemblages of tales previously handed down orally over many generations. Many are contemporary with the creation of the Kailas, and thus, like the temple itself, are products of (or perhaps an impetus for) Hinduism's great popular surge in the middle centuries of that millennium.
11. Soar, Micaela. "The Tirtha at Ellora". In *Ellora Caves: Sculptures and Architecture*. Collected papers of the University Grants Commission's National Seminar. New Delhi: Books & Books, 1988: p. 103.
12. Berkson, Carmel. *Ellora, Concept and Style*. New Delhi: Abhinav, 1992: p. 45.
13. Kramrisch 1946, *Op. cit.*, p. 357.
    Here she speaks generally, and not in reference to any specific Hindu temple. Her description here, however, applies particularly well to the Kailas.
14. Coomaraswamy 1995, *Op. cit.*, p.105.
15. Baumer, Bettina. "From Guha to Akasha: The Mystic Cave in Vedic and Saiva Traditions". In *Ellora Caves: Sculptures and Architecture*. Collected papers of the University Grants Commission's National Seminar. New Delhi: Books & Books, 1988: p. 61.
16. *Ibid.*, p.69.
17. Kramrisch 1946, *Op. cit.*, p.180.
18. Narzary, pp, 121-2.
19. Baumer 1988, *Op. cit.*, p. 62.
20. *Ibid.*, p.63. The five elements of the material universe are earth, water, air, fire, and space.
21. *Ibid.*, quoting from the "fundamental text" of the Taittiriya Upanishad (II:I): "He who knows Brahman attains the supreme. As has been said: Brahman is Reality, Wisdom, Infinity, he who knows it as hidden in the cave [of the heart] and placed in the highest heaven, attains all desires together with the wise Brahman."
22. *Ibid.*, p. 65, quoting from the Chandogya Upanishad.
23. *Ibid.*, p. 77.

BIBLIOGRAPHY

Ashby, Philip H. *Modern Trends in Hinduism*. New York: Columbia University Press, 1960.

Banerjea, Jitendra Nath. *The Development of Hindu Iconography*. New Delhi: Munshiram Manoharlal, 1956.

Baumer, Bettina. "From Guha to Akasha: The Mystic Cave in Vedic and Saiva Traditions". In *Ellora Caves: Sculptures and Architecture*. Collected papers of the University Grants Commission's National Seminar. New Delhi: Books & Books, 1988.

Berkson, Carmel. *Ellora, Concept and Style*. New Delhi: Abhinav, 1992.

Berkson, Carmel. *The Divine and the Demoniac*. Calcutta: Oxford India, 1997.

Bhattacharya, Asok K. "Ellora Sculpture: A Stylistic Examination". In *Ellora Caves: Sculptures and Architecture*. Collected papers of the University Grants Commission's National Seminar. New Delhi: Books & Books, 1988.

Brrodbeck, Simon. *Introduction to the Bhagavad Gita*. London: Penguin, 1962.

Brown, Percy. *Indian Architecture (Buddhist and Hindu Periods)*. Reprint, Bombay: Taraporevala, 1965.

Burgess, James and James Fergusson. *The Cave Temples of India*. 1880. Reprint, Delhi: Oriental Books, 1965.

Coomaraswamy, Ananda K. *History of Indian and Indonesian Art*. New York: Dover, 1927.

Coomaraswamy, Ananda K. *The Dance of Shiva*. Reprint, New Delhi: Sagar, 1968.

Coomaraswamy, Ananda K. *Introduction to Indian Art*. Reprint, New Delhi: Munshiram Manoharlal, 1968.

Coomaraswamy, Ananda K. *Essays in Architectural Theory*, ed. Michael Meister. Oxford University Press, 1969.

Czuma, Stanislaw Jerzy. "The Brahmanical Rashtrakuta Monuments of Ellora". Ph.D sissertation, University of Michigan, 1968.

Dallapiccola, Anna L. *Dictionary of Hindu Lore and Legend*. London: Thames & Hudson, 2002.

Deshpande, M. N. "Kailasa: A Study in its Symbolism". In *Ellora Caves: Sculptures and Architecture*. Collected papers of the University Grants Commission's National Seminar. New Delhi: Books & Books, 1988.

Dhavalikar, M. K. "Kailasa – The Stylistic Development and Chronology". In *Bulletin of the Deccan College Research Institute* 41, (1982): pp. 33–45.

Dhavalikar, M. K. "Kailasa – A Structural Analysis". In *Ellora Caves: Sculptures and Architecture*. Collected papers of the University Grants Commission's National Seminar. New Delhi: Books & Books, 1988.

Dhavalikar, M. K. *Masterpieces of Rashtrakuta Art*. Bombay: Taraporevala, 1983.

Dimmitt, Cornelia and J.A.B van Buitenen (ed.). *Classical Hindu Mythology: A Reader in the Sanskrit Puranas*. Philadelphia: Temple University Press, 1978.

Eck, Diana L. *Darshan: Seeing the Divine in India*. Chambersburg PA: Anima, 1985.

Eck, Diana L. *India: A Sacred Geography*. New York: Harmony Books, 2012.

Fergusson, James. *History of Indian and Eastern Architecture*. 1876. Reprint, revised & edited by James Burgess, Delhi: Munshiram Manoharlal, 1967.

Frederic, Louis. *The Art of India: Temples and Sculpture*. New York: Abrams, 1969.

Goetz, Hermann. "The Kailasa of Ellora and the Chronology of Rashtrakuta Art". In *Artibus Asiae* 15, (1952): pp. 84–107.

Goetz, Hermann. *The Art of India*. New York: Crown, 1964.

Gold, Ann Grodzins. *Fruitful Journeys: The Ways of Rajasthani Pilgrims*. Berkeley: University of California Press, 1988.

Gupte, Ramesh and B. D. Mahajan. *Ajanta, Ellora and the Aurangabad Caves*. Bombay: Taraporevala, 1962.

Hardy, Adam. *Indian Temple Architecture: Form and Transformation*. New Delhi: Abhinav, 1995.

Hawley, John Stratton. "Scenes from the Childhood of Krishna on the Kailasanatha Temple, Ellora". In *Archives of Asian Art* 34 (1981): pp. 74–90.

Heston, Mary Beth. "Iconographic Themes of the Gopura of the Kailasanatha Temple at Ellora". In *Artibus Asiae* Vol. 43 No. 3 (1981/82): pp. 219–235.

Ions, Veronica. *Indian Mythology*. London: Paul Hamlyn, 1967.

Jeyechandrun, A. V. "Dravidian Influence on Ellora Cave Temple Architecture". In *Ellora Caves: Sculptures and Architecture*. Collected papers of the University Grants Commission's National Seminar. New Delhi: Books & Books, 1988.

Kakar, Sudhir. *Intimate Relations: Exploring Indian Sexuality*. University of Chicago Press, 1989.

Kramrisch, Stella. *The Hindu Temple*. 1946. Reprint, Delhi: Motilal Banarsidass, 1976.

Kramrisch, Stella. *The Presence of Shiva*. Princeton University Press, 1981.

Malandra, Geri H. "The Creation of a Past for Ajanta and Ellora". In *Perceptions of South Asia's Visual Past*, eds. Catherine B. Ayer and Thomas Metcalf. New Delhi: Oxford, 1994.

Markel, Stephen. "The Ramayana Cycle on the Kailasanatha Temple at Ellora". *Ars Orientalis Supplement* 1 (2000): pp. 59–71.

Meister, Michael W. "Vastupurusamandalas: Planning in the Image of Man". In *Mandalas and Yantras in the Hindu Tradition*, ed. Gudrun Bühnemann. Brill, Boston and Leiden, 2002: pp. 251–270.

Menon, Ramesh. *The Ramayana*. New York: North Point Press, 2001.

Michell, George. *The Hindu Temple: An Introduction to Its Meaning and Forms*. New York: Harper & Row, 1977.
Michell, George. *The Penguin Guide to the Monuments of India*, Vol. 1. London: Viking, 1989.

Narzary, Janak Jhankar. A Hindu View of Unity: Its impact on the Styles of Hindu Sculpture. In *Ellora Caves: Sculptures and Architecture*. Collected papers of the University Grants Commission's National Seminar. New Delhi: Books & Books, 1988.

O'Flaherty, Wendy Doniger. *The Rig Veda*. London: Penguin, 1961.

Pandya, Yatin. *Concepts of Space in Traditional Indian Architecture*. Ahmedabad: Mapin, 2005.

Parimoo, Ratan et al. *Ellora Caves: Sculptures and Architecture*. Collected papers of the University Grants Commission's National Seminar. New Delhi: Books & Books, 1988.

Roebuck, Valerie J. *The Upanishads*. London: Penguin, 2003.

Rowland, Benjamin. *The Art & Architecture of India: Buddhist/Hindu/Jain*. Baltimore: Penguin, 1967.

Seely, Captain John B. *The Wonders of Ellora*. London: G. & A. Whitaker, 1824.

Sen Gupta, R. "The Panels of Kalyanasundramurti at Ellora". In *Lalit Kala* 7 (1960): pp. 14–18.

Sivaramamurti, Calambur. *The Art of India*. New York: Abrams, 1977.

Soar, Micaela. "The Tirtha at Ellora". In *Ellora Caves: Sculptures and Architecture*. Collected papers of the University Grants Commission's National Seminar. New Delhi: Books & Books, 1988.

Soar, Micaela. "Ellora". Entry in *Grove's Dictionary of Art*, ed. Jane Turner. New York, Macmillan (1996): pp 147–150.

Soundara Rajan, K. V. *The Ellora Monoliths*. Delhi: Gian, 1988.

Soundara Rajan, K. V. "Keynote Address". In *Ellora Caves: Sculptures and Architecture*. Collected papers of the University Grants Commission's National Seminar. New Delhi: Books & Books, 1988.

Soundara Rajan, K. V. *Rock Cut Temple Styles*. Mumbai: Somaiya, 1990.

Spink, Walter. *Ajanta to Ellora*. Bombay and Ann Arbor: Marg Publications, 1967.

Walker, Benjamin. *Hindu World*. London: George Allen & Unwin, 1968.

Zimmer, Heinrich. *Philosophies of India* , ed. Joseph Campbell. New York: Pantheon, 1951.

Zimmer, Heinrich. *The Art of Indian Asia* (completed and edited by Joseph Campbell). Princeton University Press: 1972.

Zimmer, Heinrich. *Myths and Symbols in Indian Art and Civilization*, ed. Joseph Campbell. Princeton University Press: 1972.

INTACH
Aurangabad

Indian National Trust for Art and Cultural Heritage

The Indian National Trust for Art and Cultural Heritage (INTACH) is a nationwide non-profit organisation founded in 1984 with the aim of protecting and conserving India's natural and cultural heritage. The headquarters of INTACH are in Delhi and it has over 140 chapters around the country. Its main activities have been in the areas of listing of heritage buildings, building conservation, heritage awareness programs, and providing conservation know-how.

INTACH Aurangabad Chapter is actively involved in conservation of historically significant buildings / structures in the Marathwada region. It has taken up a project with the help of Aurangabad Municipal Corporation to carry out conservation and beautification of the 400-year-old gates for which Aurangabad city is so well known. The Chapter is also helping the District Administration to put up signage at various historical sites and with conservation and beautification of Nagarkhana gate near Khultabad. INTACH Aurangabad Chapter also regularly brings out publications, like the excellent field guide *Aurangabad: Art, Culture, Architecture* (2010), to create awareness about the rich heritage of the region among the local residents and tourists.